COMBAT AIRCRAFT

156 RAF JAGUAR UNITS IN COMBAT

SERIES EDITOR TONY HOLMES

156

COMBAT AIRCRAFT

Michael Napier

RAF JAGUAR UNITS IN COMBAT

OSPREY

PUBLISHING

OSPREY PUBLISHING
Bloomsbury Publishing Plc
Kemp House, Chawley Park, Cumnor Hill, Oxford OX2 9PH, UK
29 Earlsfort Terrace, Dublin 2, Ireland
1385 Broadway, 5th Floor, New York, NY 10018, USA
E-mail; info@ospreypublishing.com
www.ospreypublishing.com

OSPREY is a trademark of Osprey Publishing Ltd

First published in Great Britain in 2025

A catalogue record for this book is available from the British Library.

ISBN PB 9781472865250; eBook 9781472865267; ePDF 9781472865274;
XML 9781472865243

25 26 27 28 29 10 9 8 7 6 5 4 3 2 1

Edited by Tony Holmes
Cover Artwork by Gareth Hector
Aircraft Profiles by Janusz Światłoń
Index by Alison Worthington
Originated by PDQ Digital Media Solutions, UK
Printed by Repro India Ltd.

Osprey Publishing supports the Woodland Trust, the UK's leading woodland
conservation charity.

To find out more about our authors and books visit **www.ospreypublishing.com**.
Here you will find extracts, author interviews, details of forthcoming events and
the option to sign up for our newsletter.

Acknowledgements
I am very grateful to the following for
their contributions to this book –
Chris Allam, Dave Bagshaw, Lee
Barton (Air Historical Branch), Ian
Black, Simon Blake, Nick Connor,
Andrew Dennis (RAF Museum), Alex
Emtage, Ian Hall (for permission to
quote from *Jaguar Boys*, published by
Grub Street in 2014), Tim Hewlett,
Tim Kerss, Andy Millikin, Alex
Muskett, Malcolm Rainier, Michael
Rondot, Pete Tholen and Shaun
Wildey.

Front Cover
Flt Lt Pete Tholen, flying Jaguar
GR 1A XZ356 on a Surface Combat Air
Patrol mission, carries out a CRV7 rocket
attack on an Iraqi Polnochny-class
amphibious warfare ship in the Persian Gulf
near Faylaka Island on 30 January 1991.
Subsequent strafing passes by Tholen and
his element leader, Wg Cdr William Pixton,
left the vessel ablaze from stem to stern
(*Cover Artwork by Gareth Hector*)

Previous Pages
A fine study of Jaguar GR 1A XZ373 in
flight over the Adriatic Sea during an
Operation *Deny Flight* sortie from Gioia Del
Colle in November 1994. The aircraft's
overwing-mounted AIM-9L AAMs and
AN/ALQ-101-10 EW pod can be clearly
seen. The Sidewinders were routinely
carried for self-defence since there was still
a potential air-to-air threat, however
remote, from Serbian aircraft (*Author's
Collection*)

CONTENTS

INTRODUCTION

An Anglo-French collaborative project, the Jaguar was produced jointly by the British Aircraft Corporation (later British Aerospace) and Breguet (later Dassault-Breguet) under the auspices of the *Société Européenne de Production de l'Avion Ecole de Combat et d'Appui Tactique* (SEPECAT). In the 1960s, it was a contemporary of two other Anglo-French aircraft projects, the Concorde supersonic airliner and the Anglo-French Variable Geometry (AFVG) strike aircraft.

The Jaguar had originally been intended as an advanced trainer and light attack aircraft, based on the Breguet 121 design, and was to be built in five variants – Jaguar A, a single-seat light attack aircraft for the French Air Force (*Armée de l'Aire* – AdA); Jaguar E, a two-seat trainer for the AdA; Jaguar B, a two-seat trainer for the Royal Air Force (RAF); Jaguar S, a single-seat ground attack aircraft for the RAF; and Jaguar M, a single-seat carrier-based strike aircraft for the French Naval Aviation (*Aéronavale*). However, after the French pulled out of the AFVG project in 1967, forcing its cancellation, the RAF reconsidered the operational requirements for Jaguar S, and it evolved into a more complex strike/attack aircraft.

The French-built prototype, a Jaguar E, first flew in September 1968, and its British counterpart, a Jaguar S, followed a year later. A total of 400 Jaguars were built, and the British and French armed services each received half of the production run. In the meantime, under pressure from

Two Jaguar GR 3s of No 6 Sqn in flight shortly before the type was withdrawn from service in May 2007. Significant updates, particularly in the last ten years of its service, had ensured that the Jaguar remained capable and effective throughout its operational life (*Crown Copyright/MoD*)

Dassault, the *Aéronavale* had changed its mind and selected the Étendard as its carrier-based strike aircraft over the Jaguar. The 50 Jaguar Ms that had been ordered by the *Aéronavale* were instead built as As for the AdA.

The RAF order was for 165 single-seat Jaguar GR 1s (Jaguar Ss) and 37 two-seat Jaguar T 2s (Jaguar Bs). The Jaguar was powered by two Rolls-Royce Turbomeca Adour 102 afterburning turbofan engines and armed with a pair of DEFA 30 mm cannon, with provision to carry weapons and stores on four underwing pylons and an under-fuselage centreline pylon. In addition, two air-to-air missiles (AAMs) could be carried on overwing pylons.

The brains of the aircraft was the sophisticated Marconi-Elliott Navigation and Weapon Aiming Sub-System (NAVWASS), which gave the pilot accurate navigation information via a projected map display and weapon aiming symbology in the Head-Up Display (HUD). In addition, a Ferranti Laser Ranger and Marked Target Seeker (LRMTS) and a Marconi ARI 18223 Radar Warning Receiver (RWR) were retrofitted to the Jaguar GR 1, which also benefitted from upgrading with the Adour 104 in 1978. With full afterburner, the new engine delivered ten per cent more power than the earlier version, giving better take-off performance. The Jaguar was capable of air-to-air refuelling (AAR) with a retractable probe fitted into the right side of the aircraft's nose.

The Jaguar entered frontline RAF service at Coltishall, in Norfolk, in 1974, replacing the Phantom FGR 2 in the ground attack role. In turn, the Phantom FGR 2s were released to replace the Lightning in the air defence role. Once fully formed, the Coltishall Wing comprised two attack squadrons and one tactical reconnaissance squadron, and was declared to the NATO Allied Command Europe Mobile Force. The three Jaguar squadrons at Coltishall also formed part of Britain's national rapid reaction force.

Meanwhile, in 1975, the Phantom FGR 2 squadrons at Brüggen, in West Germany, began to re-equip with the new type. The Jaguar Wing at Brüggen comprised four squadrons in the nuclear strike and conventional attack roles, which were declared to the NATO Allied Air Forces Central Europe (AAFCE) 2nd Tactical Air Force. A tactical reconnaissance squadron was also based in West Germany, at Laarbruch. By 1977, the Air Order of Battle of the RAF Jaguar Force was as follows:

RAF Strike Command	
No 38 Group	
Coltishall	No 6 Sqn
	No 41 Sqn (reconnaissance)
	No 54 Sqn

RAF Germany	
Brüggen	No 14 Sqn
	No 17 Sqn
	No 20 Sqn
	No 31 Sqn
Laarbruch	No 2 Sqn (reconnaissance)

The prime role of the Brüggen Wing was nuclear strike using the British WE177 weapon. The Jaguar was the first single-seat aircraft to be employed in this role, and since all procedures in relation to nuclear weapons are based on the 'two-man principle' in which no single person has access to a weapon system, extra measures were needed to ensure the integrity of the processes. At Brüggen, five nuclear-armed aircraft were continuously maintained on Quick Reaction Alert at 15 minutes readiness to launch throughout the Jaguar years. The RAF Germany-based Jaguars were also fully integrated into the AAFCE conventional (i.e. non-nuclear) 'Option Alpha', which comprised pre-planned attacks on Warsaw Pact airfields and strategic surface-to-air (SAM) systems.

Another 'first' achieved at Brüggen was operation from Hardened Aircraft Shelters (HASs), which were constructed at the base in the mid-1970s. HAS operations ensured that the Wing could continue to fly combat missions during Nuclear, Biological and Chemical threats, as well as protecting the aircraft from air and missile attack. A tough regime of frequent no-notice exercises, including periodic Tactical Evaluations by

A Jaguar GR 1A of No 17 Sqn flies over the Kerspe Dam near Remscheid in Germany. The prime role of the Jaguar Wing at Brüggen during the Cold War was low-level nuclear strike. At its height in the late 1970s and early 1980s, the Jaguar force consisted of eight squadrons (*Crown Copyright/MoD*)

AAFCE staff, ensured that the Brüggen Wing maintained the highest levels of readiness and combat effectiveness.

At Laarbruch, No 2 Sqn carried out the reconnaissance role using the bespoke EMI Jaguar reconnaissance pod. The latter was optimised for low-level operations, with one forward-looking camera and a fan of four more cameras giving 120-degree coverage on either side and beneath the aircraft. Additionally, an infra-red linescan was located in the rear of the pod. Pilots carried out visual reconnaissance to supplement the photographs and in case there was any failure within the pod.

Wartime tasking from the Combined Air Operations Centre would mostly be reactive, but there were also four pre-planned reconnaissance programmes covering the expected axes of advance by Warsaw Pact forces. The Jaguar reconnaissance pod could also be configured for medium-level operations using an F126 camera in the front section. The Jaguar began to be withdrawn from RAF Germany in 1984, when the aircraft at Brüggen and Laarbruch were progressively replaced by the Tornado GR 1. By the time the last Jaguar unit in RAF Germany, No 2 Sqn, re-equipped with the Tornado GR 1A in January 1989, the Jaguar force comprised just the three squadrons at Coltishall. The Air Order of Battle of the RAF Jaguar force in 1989 was as follows:

RAF Strike Command	
No 1 Group	
Coltishall	No 6 Sqn
	No 41 Sqn (reconnaissance)
	No 54 Sqn

In contrast to the RAF Germany-based squadrons, the Coltishall Wing did not have a nuclear role, concentrating instead on mobile operations. In wartime, the attack squadrons would be expected to deploy to Tirstrup, in Denmark, and the reconnaissance squadron to Bardufoss, in Norway, and all three units frequently practised deployments to these bases at short notice. Being a relatively simple aircraft, the Jaguar was well suited to this role, since it required little external support and was very serviceable. A mobile Reconnaissance Interpretation Centre accompanied deployments by No 41 Sqn.

After the Cold War, the well-proven capability of the Coltishall Jaguar Wing to react quickly in times of crisis meant that the aircraft was the first RAF offensive support type to be sent to the Middle East in 1990 prior to the first Gulf War, to Turkey for operations over northern Iraq in 1991 and to Italy for operations over the Balkans in 1993.

Throughout its service life the Jaguar received upgrades to improve its effectiveness. In 1983 the fleet was modified to GR 1A standard with the replacement of the original Elliott E3B inertial platform within the NAVWASS with the Ferranti FIN 1064. Apart from offering a significantly better navigation platform, this modification also introduced improved ergonomics by moving the NAVWASS controls onto the cockpit coaming so that the pilot did not have to go 'heads in' when making selections on the control panel.

The upgrade programme also included the procurement of Electronic Warfare (EW) equipment in the shape of the AN/ALQ-101-10 jamming pod and Phimat chaff dispenser, as well as the fitting of a chaff dispenser in place of the landing parachute in the tail cone. The EW pods were carried on the outer underwing pylons, leaving the inner underwing and fuselage centreline pylons available for fuel drop tanks, weapons or a reconnaissance pod. Two 1200-litre fuel tanks could be carried on the underwing pylons, with a reconnaissance pod or bombs on the centreline pylon, or a single tank could be carried on the centreline, with weapons loaded on the underwing pylons.

Recognising the need for a precision strike capability for the Jaguar after the Gulf War, the RAF had 11 aircraft modified under an Urgent Operational Requirement (UOR) in 1994 to carry the GEC-Ferranti Thermal Imaging Airborne Laser Designator (TIALD) pod, becoming the GR 1B variant. In this modification, a Military Standard 1553B databus was fitted as well as a new HUD and controls for the pod itself.

A further enhancement programme three years later, known as 'Jaguar 96', modernised the remaining Jaguar GR 1A and T 2 fleet, now numbering some 60 airframes, to the Jaguar GR 3 and T 4 standard, respectively. Most of the GR 1B modifications were incorporated (although not all GR 3 aircraft were TIALD capable), as well as Hands On Throttle And Stick controls for avionics and weapons functions and full compatibility with Night Vision Goggles. The programme also featured a global positioning system (GPS) feed to the navigation/attack system and a terrain-matching database for the TERPROM ground proximity warning system.

A final upgrade of 36 aircraft under the 'Jaguar 97' project to become Jaguar GR 3As was rolled out in 2002. Along with various avionic enhancements, the aircraft were re-fitted with more powerful Adour 106 engines and equipped with a Helmet Mounted Sight System.

After almost continuous operations over Iraq and the Balkans since 1990, the Jaguar force was due to participate in Operation *Telic* (the Second Gulf War) in 2003. The plan was for eight Jaguars operating from the Turkish airfield at Incirlik to support an advance southwards from Turkey, but when the Turkish government vetoed this idea, the Jaguars were replaced by Harrier GR 7s operating from bases in Kuwait and Jordan.

Although it was largely withdrawn from deployments to Iraq and Afghanistan after 2004, the Jaguar force continued to contribute to the success of those operations by training Forward Air Controllers (FACs) in preparation for their overseas tours.

With increasing financial pressure on the defence budget, the Jaguar force began to be run down with the disbandment of No 54 Sqn on 11 March 2005. No 41 Sqn followed on 1 April 2006, transferring all of its aircraft to No 6 Sqn, which moved to Coningsby, in Lincolnshire, on the same day. The original plan was for No 6 Sqn to continue flying the Jaguar until 2009 but, with just a month's notice, the unit ceased flying on 30 May 2007 and was formally disbanded the following day. At the final parade, the squadron commander, Wg Cdr John Sullivan, said 'It's with great regret that I have to concede the Jaguar has come to the end of its service life. It's still a very capable platform and has some unique capabilities that are not yet fielded by any other aircraft out there – so it is with frustration the end has come. I'm proud that the Jaguar is going out at the pinnacle of its capability.'

CHAPTER ONE

IRAQ – OPERATION *GRANBY*

8 August 1990–16 January 1991

Newly painted in 'Desert Pink' ARTF paint and laden down with three 1200-litre external fuel tanks, Jaguar GR 1A XX112 taxis out at Coltishall at the start of its deployment to Thumrait on 11 August 1990. A Phimat chaff pod can is mounted on the outboard wing pylon. This aircraft was later modified to GR 3A standard and still survives as an instructional airframe at Cosford (*Crown Copyright/RAF Museum*)

The Berlin Wall fell at the end of 1989, marking the end of the Cold War, and, for the first time in four decades, leaving the air forces in Europe suddenly without a clearly defined enemy. However, a new adversary was not long in coming forward. Smarting from the disastrous nine-year war with Iran, the Ba'athist regime in Iraq attempted to recover some of its lost prestige by resurrecting the nation's territorial claims over neighbouring Kuwait. Using the accusation of slant drilling by Kuwait into the Rumayla oilfield as an excuse, Iraq invaded its neighbour on 2 August 1990, precipitating an international crisis. Determined first to protect the sovereignty of Saudi Arabia, and then to liberate Kuwait, the USA sent a task force to the Gulf region and began to assemble an international Coalition.

The British government approved military participation on 8 August 1990 and a warning order was issued to the Coltishall Wing to prepare eight attack and four reconnaissance Jaguars to be at 24 hours' readiness to move. The detachment was to be stocked with sufficient weapons for five days of offensive operations. The aircraft were selected from across the wing and sprayed with 'Desert Pink' Alkaline-Removable Temporary Finish (ARTF) paint. The painting was carried out overnight on 10–11 August by station personnel augmented by the local Air Training Corps.

Meanwhile, 24 pilots, drawn from across the wing, as well as some 300 groundcrew, had been selected for deployment under the command of Wg Cdr Jerry Connolly (OC No 6 Sqn).

'The pilots going to the Gulf were selected based on experience from both Nos 6 and 54 Sqns, No 41 Sqn being in the USA on a recce exercise', explained Flt Lt Nick Connor. 'Ironically, when the war started, it was No 41 Sqn, plus the least experienced pilots, plus pilots from the Operational Conversion Unit, who did the fighting because our detachment had rolled home prior to Christmas!

'I was the Qualified Weapons Instructor [QWI] on No 54 Sqn when the news of the invasion broke. We started a few rushed days of intensive Operational Low Flying down at 100 ft in Scotland whilst preparing for possible deployment. This was essentially a quick refresher, as the squadron had only recently returned from Exercise Maple Flag in Canada.

'The aircraft were being quickly "improved", including the removal of the head-up warning panel next to the HUD and a quick paint job in "Desert Pink". This was only finished hours before departure, and it was a rushed job – I recall getting in the cockpit and having to scrape overspray off some of the instruments! The story goes that the paint had not been used for many years, and had to be collected from somewhere in the UK. The driver, still in peacetime mode, had to stop for his "rest break", and so it arrived late in the evening the day before deployment. So rushed was it that the radomes of the ECM pods were pink as well, and this was only scraped off once we got to the Gulf.'

Flt Lt Connor's predecessor as squadron QWI, Flt Lt Alex Muskett, was also selected for the initial deployment;

'I had just started language training prior to commencing an exchange tour with the Royal Netherlands Air Force. I hadn't flown since 5 July, but when I heard Jaguars were to deploy to the region I called my boss, OC No 54 Sqn, Wg Cdr "Dim" Jones, and offered my services. On 9 August I was told to jump into a Jaguar GR 1A and get myself current. After a couple of OLF [Operational Low Flying] Simulated Attack Profile sorties later that day, and a further one the next day, I found myself strapped into Jaguar XX741 on 11 August ready to depart to Akrotiri [on Cyprus].

'If we hadn't considered how serious this was before, the issue of a Walther PP and a plastic bag of ammunition as we left the Squadron Operations Desk drove it home that this was no ordinary deployment. No 6 Sqn was the lead unit, and its engineers, along with help no doubt from across the Station, and fortified by copious amounts of tea served up by Air Cadets on their summer camp, had done a sterling job to prepare 12 aircraft, including painting them a very fetching shade of pink.'

On 11 August the 12 Jaguars departed Coltishall in three waves, each of four aircraft. 'It was a sobering experience', recalled Connor, 'and I remember looking back at the UK in its summer glory wondering what was ahead, and if we would see it again. It is hard now to appreciate the different situation in the Middle East in 1990, but Iraq at the time was said to have 600 combat aircraft and one million men under arms. As Cold War pilots, this was definitely "new territory", as evidenced by the fact that the moving map stopped somewhere near Cyprus! Not that that

Jaguar GR 1A XZ355 lands at Thumrait after a training sortie over Oman. In the early days of the detachment, the emphasis was on ultra-low-level flying. This aircraft has an AN/ALQ-101-10 jamming pod on its outboard wing pylon. XZ355 is now owned by a private collector in Greece (*US National Archive*)

was significant because when it did turn up again, it was, as you might expect, showing a barren, featureless desert!'

Each wave was supported by a VC10K tanker for the flight to Akrotiri, where the Jaguars waited for their final destination to be confirmed. After spending another day in Cyprus, the aircraft flew on to Thumrait, in Oman, on 13 August, accompanied this time by TriStar tankers. At the same time, the remaining members of the detachment flew out to Oman in VC10 and Hercules transports. 'I had a refuelling probe fault that resulted in it being half retracted', continued Connor, 'but luckily it was after the last top up. When we reached Thumrait, I remember being surprised at the need for a bit of burner on finals as it was so hot. It was very reassuring to get there and see about 20 F-15Es who had tanked direct from Seymour Johnson AFB in North Carolina, and to find that they were the same guys who we had been with us at Maple Flag three months prior'.

The following day (14 August), four Jaguars loaded with BL755 cluster bomb units and full guns manned the quick reaction alert at Thumrait, ready to respond to any tasking. In the initial phase of the detachment, the aircraft were modified to a standard known as Stage 1, which involved the fitting of a HaveQuick secure radio and a Mk 12 Mode 4 IFF transponder. Tracor AN/ALE-40 flare dispensers were also scabbed onto the rear of the lower fuselage and the engine turbine temperature limits were increased to give better take-off performance in the heat.

Thumrait had been chosen since it was home to the Jaguars of No 8 Sqn of the Sultan of Oman's Air Force (SOAF). However, it was more than 1000 miles from Iraq, which meant the base was far from convenient for launching missions into Iraq or the Kuwaiti Theatre of Operations (KTO). Nevertheless, it proved to be an ideal location for carrying out an operational work-up for the pilots, and a vigorous training regime was started. Four- and six-ship formations flew missions with the USAF F-15E Strike Eagles and SOAF Jaguars that were co-located at Thumrait. The Jaguar pilots practised ultra-low-level (ULL) flying and used the air weapons ranges at Aqzayl and Rubcut to perfect their weapon delivery technique. Initially, 12 training sorties were planned for each day, but that was soon increased to 16 and then eventually 24 sorties per day.

Seen immediately post-war during a training mission from Coltishall, this aircraft is expending flares from its twin AN/ALE-40 dispensers mounted just forward of the ventral strakes. The dispensers were scabbed onto the aircraft as part of the Stage 1 modification to Jaguars sent to Thumrait in August 1990 (*Ian Black*)

'The flying was very low', confirmed Flt Lt Nick Connor. 'We got down to about 20–30 ft sustained, but in the end settled at about 70 ft so you could actually look out. I recall the "bounce" [intercepting Jaguar] one day telling us to back off the ULL because he had seen a wingtip just feet off the ground when a Jag was turning. The Jag managed about 450 knots, unlike the more usual 540 knots or so in max dry, due to the heat, and the laser chisel windows [in the nose] were opaque after about a month due to sand blasting.

'When flying, my green issue helmet was so hot due to the sun you could not hold your hand on it for more than a few seconds – that is why they were all painted sand brown ASAP. All this sort of stuff was just decided at squadron level and the next minute it was done, which was quite refreshing after the normal very slow RAF process in the UK. At this time, we got new "secret" anti-dazzle laser visors, but I do remember that they made depth perception a bit strange for me – not ideal at 70 ft! We also obtained/borrowed from the USAF infra-red strobes to go in the life jackets to help location in the event of ejection.

'It was frustrating that one F-15E could do the work of three Jags at night and then swing to the air-to-air role – I recall that their standard load was four AIM-7, four AIM-9s and eight CBUs [cluster bomb units] or 500-lb bombs. When I asked one of their pilots if they had made any modifications for the war, I was told, "Nope, they figured we did not need any" – how very USAF and non-RAF!'

While the search continued for a better location from an operational perspective, the pilots realised that the tactical situation in the KTO lent itself more to medium-level operations than low-level flying. The problem was that their main weapons – BL755 and 30 mm cannon – could only be employed from low-level.

'Training had commenced in earnest, with the initial emphasis on ULL flying and range work', recalled Flt Lt Muskett. 'Often, we were so low that flares barely had time to ignite before impacting the desert floor. Clearly, as the initial response was expected to be against an armoured invasion, low-level was our only real choice as the BL755 CBUs we had couldn't be delivered from medium-level, but our thoughts soon turned to exploring what we could do from medium-level.

'We started practising dive attacks from 15,000–20,000 ft at Aqzayl range using 14 kg practice bombs, but immediately discovered we had an issue with weapon aiming. Whichever ranging option we employed, laser or barometric, the accuracy was extremely variable, with some weapons falling short by a half-mile or more. This was fed back to the UK, where analysis of the aircraft's system highlighted that the atmospheric model it used was optimised for the lower altitudes at which it was expected to operate – hence its lack of any sort of accuracy from medium-level. Eventually, a "frig" was introduced in time for the commencement of operations in January 1991 whereby the target's height was adjusted to compensate for the inaccurate atmospheric model, making realistic medium-level operations possible.

'The strafe profile was modified with a pop up to about 1100 ft and then a dive. During this pre-war period it was all a bit manic to be honest, and the revised strafing profile was backed off a bit when one of the boys firing High Explosive [HE] shells saw a car door in the air out of the window – our targets were old cars, trucks, etc. I witnessed such attacks from the range tower, and noticed that in some cases, because the angle of attack was so low, the rounds went a long way down-range up to perhaps a half-mile or so to explode when impacting on a low cliff! For a few days pilots were even practising strafe pop ups out in the desert on old oil drums, but this soon stopped as it was considered a bit risky, and someone mentioned they might be owned by the local Bedouin tribe.

'We also started trying to gain experience with CRV7 rockets whilst here, as the Omanis were potential customers so there were some on base. It was a crazy all rules out the window period.'

Experimenting with Bristol Aerospace CRV7 rockets proved prescient, for the RAF was already looking into the possibility of acquiring the weapon but the procurement process was painfully slow. On the same day that the Jaguars deployed to Thumrait, staff at the Ministry of Defence had prompted British Aerospace to complete a feasibility study into carriage of the weapon on the Jaguar. The results of the study were to hand by the end of August, but an Operational Emergency Clearance to use the weapon would not be issued until 21 December. Nevertheless, the ad hoc trial by the Thumrait detachment had given the Jaguar force at least some experience with the weapon.

Meanwhile, as well as honing their tactical flying skills, the Jaguar pilots had to deal with the challenges of desert living. Flt Lt Nick

At Thumrait, the Jaguar Detachment (JagDet) shared the ramp with F-15E Strike Eagles of the 4th Tactical Fighter Wing from Seymour Johnson AFB. The JagDet trained with both F-15Es and the resident Jaguars of the SOAF's No 8 Sqn. The aircraft in the foreground, Jaguar XX719, was transferred to the SOAF in 1998 (*US National Archive*)

Connor reported that 'about 25 per cent of the detachment went down with Shigella dysentery at one time, almost making the whole detachment inoperative. The reason was poor hygiene in the mobile field support kitchens – with temperatures at 50 degrees, the washing of aluminium mess tins in one dustbin of dodgy water was a bad idea! Soon afterwards, the treasury loosened the purse strings, allowing local commanders to spend money on paper plates that could be thrown away after use.

'Our next medical event was also self-inflicted. RAF intel briefs at the time were at four-hour intervals, and usually ended with the statement, "No attack is expected in the next four hours". When it was decided that all pilots needed jabs, they were given in the thigh muscle, with the result that most pilots were hobbling for 48 hours, remembering that "no attack is expected in the next four hours". Classic.'

Despite all the frustrations, there were lighter moments, too. According to Connor, 'If one event sums up this whole time it was a visit from the top brass and the Minister of State for the Armed Forces, Archie Hamilton, about two weeks after we got to Thumrait. The Gulfstream landed and the generals and the MP got out. Archie was welcomed by the Boss, Wg Cdr Jerry Connolly, and informed that we had eight attack and four reconnaissance Jags. Archie replied with, "Ah, reconnaissance eh . . . where does the chap with the camera sit? In the back?"'

In October an agreement was reached to redeploy the Jaguar detachment to Muharraq air base in Bahrain. The Jaguars joined a larger detachment of RAF aircraft that had been established there, including Tornado GR 1s (see *Osprey Combat Aircraft 138 – RAF Tornado Units of Gulf War 1* for details) and Victor K 2s. At some 200 miles from Kuwait, Bahrain was a much better base than Thumrait from which to strike at Iraqi forces. Critically, as it became obvious that all the AAR resources would probably be needed for deep strike missions, the Jaguar could fly sorties into Kuwait without refuelling – and that, in turn, meant that all of the Jaguar tasking would be within the KTO.

'On 7 October we deployed north to Bahrain, from where the Jaguars would eventually operate', Flt Lt Muskett later wrote. 'Targeting had changed from armour to more fixed sites – a Silkworm SSM [surface-to-

A Jaguar GR 1A taxies out at Muharraq for a training sortie during the run up to the Gulf War. A VC10K tanker is partially visible in the far left of the photograph. Tanker support enabled the JagDet to use both Saudi and Omani low-flying areas for their combat work-up (*Crown Copyright/MoD*)

In Bahrain the Coalition air forces shared the airport with civilian airliners, which continued to fly their scheduled routes throughout Operation *Granby*. Here, Jaguar GR 1A XX754 waits for a Gulf Air L-1011 TriStar to land before it can take off for a training sortie. XX754 was destroyed in a crash at low-level on 13 November 1990 and the pilot, Flt Lt Keith Collister, was killed (*Malcolm Rainier*)

surface] system on the coast of Kuwait and an ammunition storage facility just west of Kuwait City'. Flt Lt Connor added, 'after the move to Bahrain, I returned to the UK as they were short of QWIs, and we continued work on the CRV7 and software update 803 to fix what we had learnt about targeting, etc.'.

While Connor left Bahrain, Flg Off Malcolm Rainier was headed the other way. 'Flg Off Nick Collins and I were sent out on 7 October 1990 to train with the No 6 Sqn detachment, prior to OC No 41 Sqn taking over in November'. By now the aircraft were being modified to Stage 3 standard, and Rainier found that 'of the Urgent Operational Requirement [UOR] upgrades, the most noticeable was the SkyGuardian RWR, which gave accurate bearing results for emitters, as opposed to the ARI 18223 version that came before, and which merely indicated the quadrant that the emitter was in. The latter simply allowed you to "die tensed up". Overwing pylons for the AIM-9Ls, colour HUD video, tweaked engines, some signature management tweaks and a slew of new weapons completed the list.

'The overwing fit was very popular, as it enabled us to carry Phimat chaff on one wing and the AN/ALQ-101-10 deception pod [bought from the US Air National Guard and cycled through the Buccaneer force] on the other, and still retain a self-defence capability. The "Desert Pink" ARTF camouflage was very successful, being adopted by all RAF aircraft in-theatre.

'Nose art began to appear due to an excess of morale on the squadron. The false canopy applied to the nose gear door was pretty effective, and

DEBBIE was painted out halfway through the conflict because she was too ugly. She was replaced by a white rose. *The GUARDIAN reader* was selected by Sqn Ldr Mike Rondot to infuriate the audience at home.'

The nose art was the work of two of the groundcrew, Cpls Paul Robins and Chris Froome, who painted designs on a growing number of aircraft over the next few months. Much of it depicted characters from the satirical comic *Viz*, which was popular reading amongst RAF personnel.

Over the course of the next two months, a 'roulement' of personnel enabled those on the initial deployment to return home for Christmas as their places were taken by fresh pilots and groundcrew. While contingency planning continued against the pre-allocated operational targets in case short-notice missions were tasked, the training commitment also continued apace as the replacement pilots found their feet in the new theatre. The emphasis was still on practising ULL flying, and an unfortunate tragedy occurred on 13 November when Flt Lt Keith Collister was killed after his Jaguar struck the ground during a six-aircraft training sortie at ULL. The light conditions at that time of day had probably caused an optical illusion that made a large sand dune ahead of him merge with another dune behind it, making it almost invisible until the last moment.

Sqn Ldr Dave Bagshaw later commented;

'As pre-planned war missions we had inherited specified low-level attacks against coastal targets in Kuwait. Our first training sorties were flown at ULL in southwest Saudi Arabia. It was on one of those that I clocked up my 4000th Jaguar hour. We learned that on every mission we would operate as part of a large "package" – 100+ aircraft – so we rehearsed being small cogs in a very big wheel. Mission format included refuelling from our Victor tankers and then joining the package at the correct place and time. Among the other players were US Marine Corps F/A-18 Hornets and USAF F-4G Phantom II *Wild Weasels* – the latter, which could detect and destroy enemy missile radars, were to be one of our most valued support assets.

'We [later] learned that we were now likely to be tasked against Iraqi artillery batteries and their supporting facilities. These were believed to possess a chemical/biological capability, which greatly concerned Coalition ground forces. After intensive tactical discussion, we concluded that for the best chance of early target identification and accuracy of weapons delivery, the steepest possible dive attack was the best option. Therefore, as the New Year dawned, we practised mainly 30-degree dive attacks to simulate dropping our World War 2-vintage bombs or CBU-87s.'

When Wg Cdr William Pixton, OC No 41 Sqn, had taken over command of the Jaguar detachment on 9 December, there was considerable debate as to whether it should plan and practise for low-level or medium-level operations. The strong argument for operating at low-level was that the pilots were trained and well-practised in low flying, that all the weapons (1000-lb HE retarded bombs, BL755 CBUs and 30 mm cannon) could only be employed from low-level delivery profiles and that the weapon-aiming computer was optimised for the low-level environment.

This pair of Jaguars was photographed by Tornado F 3 pilot Flt Lt Ian Black during a training sortie off the Saudi Arabian coast before the conflict. In the build-up to hostilities there was much debate as to whether the Jaguars should stay with the familiar low-level tactics or move to medium-level. The overland haze clearly visible here would often complicate target acquisition during combat missions. Both of these aircraft later featured nose art and extensive mission tallies (*Ian Black*)

Furthermore, while the 1000-lb bomb could be dropped 'slick' from medium-level by disabling the retard tail and the CBU-87 might become available, the latter weapon would have to be aimed using reversionary techniques rather than computer-calculated aiming, since there would be no ballistics for the CBU-87 in the weapon-aiming computer. Operating at medium-level would also put the aircraft into the heart of the envelope for heavy Anti-Aircraft Artillery (AAA) and radar-guided SAMs such as the SA-6.

However, the counterargument ran that at low-level there would be considerable risk from light AAA, man-portable air defence systems (MANPADS) and small arms fire, and the flat desert would provide no cover to hide behind. On the other hand, the USAF *Wild Weasel* suppression of enemy air defence (SEAD) aircraft would be able to neutralise the medium-level threats.

In regard to this latter point, some pilots were sent to talk with the USAF *Wild Weasel* squadrons based nearby in Bahrain at Shaikh Isa air base. In the words of one pilot, 'it didn't take long for them to convince us that we would be mad to go in at low-level'. Another benefit of flying at medium-level would be a lighter fuel burn, which in turn would give the pilots more tactical flexibility. After listening to and considering all points of view, Pixton made the decision that the Jaguar detachment would pursue the medium-level options. It was a decision that was to prove very wise.

Meanwhile, intensive training within constituted four-ships continued in earnest. Throughout the coming conflict, pilots would fly as much as possible within the same group of four.

CHAPTER TWO

IRAQ – OPERATION *GRANBY*

17–31 January 1991

The deadline set in United Nations (UN) Security Council Resolution 678 for Iraq to withdraw from Kuwait expired on 15 January 1991, and Coalition forces were brought to full war readiness the next day. For RAF aircrew in Bahrain there was a briefing from the detachment commander. 'The pre-match briefing on the evening of 16 January was a sobering affair', Flg Off Malcolm Rainier recalled. 'The Tornado boys were to penetrate at low-level at night all the way to Saddam's strategic assets. The Jags were to be tasked in daylight over the most heavily defended part of the KTO, without dedicated SEAD. I remember murmuring to one of my friends on No 15 Sqn, which was co-located at Muharraq, that I was "glad I'm not a Tornado mate". He looked at me seriously and said, "glad I'm not a Jag mate".'

The Coalition air campaign started in the early hours of 17 January, and during the mid-morning the first Jaguar operation was launched. Mission 4451J was tasked against a police post on the Kuwaiti border that was being used by the Iraqi army as a barracks. Like all subsequent missions flown in the KTO, it was supported by US SEAD and electronic warfare (EW) aircraft, and fighter cover was also present.

Sqn Ldr Mike Gordon led Flt Lts Steve Thomas and Roger Crowder and Flg Off Malcolm Rainier on their first war sortie. 'I was fortunate enough

A pair of Jaguars in typical configuration after the first few days of the war – the aircraft carry a centreline tank, leaving the underwing pylons free to carry twice the weapon load that could be carried beneath the fuselage. AN/ALE-40 flare dispensers are just visible in front of the ventral strakes on both aircraft (*Ian Black*) to be on the first raid as part of my dedicated four-ship', continued Rainier. 'We carried two 1000-lb bombs each fitted with a Mk 960 Multi-Function Bomb Fuse (MFBF), plus two ADEN 30 mm cannon loaded with belts of 120 rounds of alternating four HE/four AP [armour-piercing] bullets. The capacity of the magazine was 150 rounds, but over-filling was known to cause stoppages, so we took 120.

'We ingressed at around 16,000 ft and egressed at around 18,000 ft – the choice of our formation leader and Flight Commander, Sqn Ldr Mike "Strike" Gordon. As he had read and understood the Air Tasking Order, and we were (correctly, as it turns out) at least as scared of our own side as the enemy, he thought we'd "go with the flow" rather than "leopard crawl" all the way to and from the target.

'We proceeded in a northerly direction, keenly listening to the newly installed and little understood SkyGuardian crystal video RWR. On the way in I saw little black puffs of smoke appearing as if by magic just to the right and below me. I was completely unprepared for the sight of AAA close by, and had to think back to war movies on a rainy afternoon to work out what I was looking at. I watched "Strike" and Steve Thomas roll in, and then it was my turn, with Roger Crowder following. Halfway down the dive the lead pairs' bombs reached the target area. They were thousands of feet short of the target (which in itself was a bit of a shock), and knowing that they would have been aiming at the right spot, I allowed my target bar to run long in an attempt to get my bombs closer to the desired mean point of impact.

'As we egressed, I was impressed at the turn of speed that the lead pair put down. It was quite a task to keep tabs on them. Roger and I closed up to do a battle-damage check on each other, and I nearly choked when I saw that he'd lost an AIM-9L from his right wing. As we taxied in at Muharraq, the rest of the team saw Roger's jet without its missile and wondered what the hell was waiting for them out there. It turned out to be a not-so-amusing (at the time) "switch pigs", which he confessed to at the debrief. As it happens, this particular "pigs" caught out a couple of other colleagues during the conflict.'

The first mission was deemed a success, with all aircraft delivering their air burst bombs accurately onto the target area.

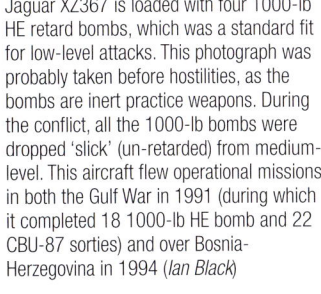

Jaguar XZ367 is loaded with four 1000-lb HE retard bombs, which was a standard fit for low-level attacks. This photograph was probably taken before hostilities, as the bombs are inert practice weapons. During the conflict, all the 1000-lb bombs were dropped 'slick' (un-retarded) from medium-level. This aircraft flew operational missions in both the Gulf War in 1991 (during which it completed 18 1000-lb HE bomb and 22 CBU-87 sorties) and over Bosnia-Herzegovina in 1994 (*Ian Black*)

The JagDet routinely flew in constituted four-ship formations. Working together in such close-knit teams ensured that the formations were as tactically efficient as possible (*Ian Black*)

The following day (18 January) saw tasking for two more Jaguar missions, but it also brought poorer weather conditions that would linger for the next few days. The first four-ship, led by Wg Cdr Bill Pixton, was tasked against vehicles and an AAA battery to the west of Kuwait City, but the pilots found that the target area was obscured by fog. Despite the weather, the AAA battery opened up and the Jaguars came under fire. Two pilots decided to drop their weapons 'blind', while the other two opted to jettison their ordnance live in the target area.

The second four-ship, which had been reduced to three aircraft after a ground abort, also found that their target was covered in mist, so they diverted to their secondary target – a storage area close to the coast in the south of the KTO. Although it too was under low cloud, the formation leader decided to release his bombs onto the target position, while his wingmen did not drop and brought their weapons back to Muharraq.

There were thick clouds at medium-level over the next few days. On 19 January eight Jaguars were tasked against three SA-2 SAM sites that had been set up in the KTO some 30 miles south of Kuwait City. Whereas Jaguars assigned to the previous missions had carried two external fuel tanks on the wing pylons and two bombs on the centreline pylon under the fuselage, on this mission each aircraft carried a single fuel tank on the centreline pylon and two 1000-lb bombs on each of the inner underwing pylons, thus doubling the weapon load.

The tactics of the day were driven by the weather conditions, and the eight aircraft flew in an extended pairs trail through dense overcast for some 40 minutes before breaking through the cloud at 15,000 ft with just a minute to run to the target area. As the Jaguars approached the target, they came under heavy AAA fire. The first four aircraft were tasked against one of the sites and the second four against the other two sites. The attack profile was a 30-degree dive, with a weapon release at around 6000 ft. Unfortunately, the leader suffered a hang-up and was unable to release his bombs, but the remaining seven pilots scored direct hits on their assigned sites. For his actions on this mission, Flg Off Malcolm Rainier was later awarded the Distinguished Flying Cross (DFC). The medal citation read;

'On 19 January 1991 whilst taking part in a coordinated eight-aircraft attack against two surface-to-air missile sites, his formation came under heavy anti-aircraft fire. Showing great presence of mind and undeterred by the obvious danger, Flying Officer Rainier promptly engaged this threat and scored a direct hit against the enemy position, eliminating the danger to the rest of the formation, who were then able to safely attack their assigned targets.'

On its return to Muharraq, one aircraft was found to have received minor damage from AAA, and the detachment commander subsequently commented that 'one experienced pilot described it as the most difficult sortie he has ever flown'.

Three more missions were launched later that day. Four Jaguars attacked an Iraqi GHN-45 155 mm howitzer battery in the southern part of the KTO, but one aircraft aborted after suffering a radio failure. The remaining three managed to find the target area despite challenging weather, but the leader could not identify the guns and dropped his bombs instead on support vehicles that were sited in berms south of the target area. The No 2 pilot did not release his bombs and returned to base with them still on board, but the No 4 pilot successfully bombed the artillery pieces.

The next four-ship, tasked against a mobile rocket launcher (MRL) battery, also had one aircraft drop out of formation, in this case due to a fuel feed problem. Once again it was not easy to identify the target in difficult conditions and under continuous AAA fire, so only the leader and the No 3 pilot bombed the target. The No 2 pilot diverted to the secondary target, but the weather in that area was even worse so he aborted, bringing his bombs back to Muharraq. Two aircraft were subsequently found to have minor AAA damage. A final four-ship also had to abort

A close-up view of the typical Operation *Granby* weapon load of two 1000-lb HE bombs carried on a tandem beam on the inboard underwing pylons, with AIM-9L Sidewinder AAMs on the overwing pylons for self-defence. A Phimat chaff dispenser pod is on the outboard pylon (*Malcolm Rainier*)

the mission because of the weather, with all the pilots returning to base with their bombs.

Another eight-ship was launched on the morning of 20 January, with each Jaguar armed with four 1000-lb bombs. For ease of control, the formation was actually flown as two four-ships, with their target being an Iraqi infantry divisional position. The first four-ship found the target obscured in fog and aborted the mission, at the same time redirecting the second four-ship to the alternative target. However, the weather at that target was also unworkable, although as they left the area the leader saw an artillery battery, which he bombed. By the time that the second four-ship began its recovery to Muharraq, the airfield was fogged in, so the formation diverted instead to Dhahran, in Saudi Arabia. Three more Jaguar missions that had been tasked that day into the KTO were cancelled because of the weather, and so too was all the tasking for 21 January.

After a delayed start on the 22nd, once again thanks to the weather, eight Jaguars were tasked against an ammunition storage area 30 miles southeast of Kuwait City. Although one aircraft ground aborted, the remaining seven found the target partially hidden under intermittent cloud cover. The formation was engaged by AAA defences, and several aircraft also received RWR indications of being locked up by an SA-2 acquisition radar. Six pilots successfully bombed the storage area and the seventh attacked the alternative target.

The day also saw the Jaguars fulfilling another role – Surface Combat Air Patrol (SUCAP). 'Every fourth trip, we were tasked to provide SUCAP', explained Flg Off Rainier, 'which involved going to a tow line out just off the coast and awaiting tasking, dipping into the AAR tow line assets when required. These missions could last up to four hours, and [later] tasks included attacking the Iraqi feint towards Khafji and sanitising the area around Failaka Island, where the US Navy lost an aircraft. We flew these as pairs, all other tasks being as dedicated four-ships'.

For the mission on 22 January, the Jaguars were loaded for the first time with CRV7 rockets, but on this day there were no targets allocated to them. Neither were there any targets assigned to either of the two SUCAP missions flown on the 23rd, but two six-aircraft missions were mounted into the KTO.

The first of these, flown in the morning, had started as an eight-ship, but two aircraft ground aborted. The target was an artillery position that included a D-30 122 mm howitzer battery and an AAA site just to the west of the Ahmad al-Jaber air base in Kuwait. In fact, the target was not at the position given in the tasking signal, but fortunately a last minute update with the correct coordinates was issued before the aircraft took off. The attack was successful and 24 1000-lb bombs were delivered onto the target.

The second six-ship of the day was launched in the afternoon against an MRL battery in a similar location to the morning target. This time the Jaguar formation was coordinated with a package of eight USAF F-16 Fighting Falcons that were to attack Ahmed al-Jaber air base itself two minutes before the Jaguars bombed their target. One F-16 was shot

A pre-war view of a pair of Jaguars refuelling from a VC10K tanker of No 101 Sqn. In practice, most of the Jaguar air interdiction and CAS missions were flown without AAR, as the aircraft could reach targets in Kuwait at medium-level without the need for additional fuel (*Malcolm Rainier*)

down during this attack, but the Jaguars obtained good hits on the rocket launchers.

By now the weather in the region had improved markedly. Clearer skies and the lessons of the previous missions drove a modification to the weapon delivery profile. By entering the dive from around 23,000 ft, the target could be acquired by 17,000–18,000 ft, with weapon release at 15,000 ft and recovery by 12,000 ft. This revised profile kept the aircraft well above the AAA fire that was now a feature of all attacks.

On the morning of 24 January, eight Jaguars were tasked against artillery positions in the southern KTO. As previously, the eight aircraft were divided into two four-ships, with one four-ship allocated an M-46 133 mm field gun battery and the second four-ship targeting a FROG-7 ballistic missile system. The Jaguars were met with a carpet of AAA that fortunately was exploding well beneath their altitude. The mission was successful, although one of the airburst-fused bombs pre-detonated (fortunately not damaging the aircraft) and another Jaguar suffered a hang-up as it attacked the FROG-7 site.

A second M-46 battery in a similar area was attacked by four Jaguars in the early afternoon. Although the leader and No 3 pilot bombed the battery successfully, the No 2 pilot was unable to see the battery because it was obscured by smoke from the leader's bombs, so he went after the alternative target – a storage facility – instead. The No 4 pilot also had problems with the attack when the computer-generated aiming in his HUD was corrupted. This incident led to an urgent request to the Central Tactics and Trials Organisation to find a solution to the problem. It was discovered that the weapon-aiming software, which had been written originally for low-level bomb delivery, had, during steep dive attacks, introduced a ten-second time delay between the pilot initiating release and the command actually being sent to the weapon pylon. It was this software 'glitch' that had caused many of the weapon hang-ups encountered on previous missions.

Meanwhile, Flt Lt Roger Crowder and Flg Off Malcolm Rainier, flying the first SUCAP mission of the day (24 January), found themselves being vectored onto two Iraqi Air Force (IrAF) Mirage F1EQs by the 'Red Crown' fighter controller aboard a Ticonderoga-class Aegis cruiser. Unfamiliar with the Jaguar, the controller was under the misapprehension that because the aircraft carried AIM-9L Sidewinder AAMs, it was an air-to-air asset.

Approaching the merge, the Jaguars descended to low-level, but in doing so they lost radio communication with the fighter controller and did not see the Mirages, which were shot down by a Royal Saudi Air Force (RSAF) F-15. Unfortunately, when the Jaguars turned southbound to return to their CAP position, the F-15 considered them potentially hostile and locked onto them. Luckily, by this stage, communications with 'Red Crown' had been restored and the F-15 was hauled off the Jaguars. Crowder then advised the controller that the Jaguars were strictly ground attack assets, and that the Sidewinders were only carried for self-defence.

On 25 January poor weather intervened once again. Mission number 4401A, comprising eight Jaguars each loaded with four 1000-lb bombs, was tasked against M-46 batteries that morning, but as the formation leader described in his after-mission report;

'Extensive cloud cover over southern Kuwait up to 15,000 ft, with isolated cumulonimbus up to 22,000 ft, precluded target identification and attack. Isolated small holes in cloud cover were used in an attempt to get through to the target, [but it was] not possible to positively identify military targets in all cases bar one.'

The leaders of each of the four-ships had aborted their attacks, but the Nos 2, 3 and 4 in the first four-ship and No 8 in the second four-ship had managed to dive through gaps in the cloud in the hope of prosecuting their attacks. Only the No 8 managed to find a military target, which he bombed.

At the same time, another pair of Jaguars was mounting a SUCAP over the Gulf. Once again, there was some confusion about the capabilities of the Jaguar on the part of the AWACS controller, who instructed the pair to climb to 44,000 ft to carry out a visual identification, little realising that this altitude was well above the practical ceiling of the aircraft in its operational fit. However, the two Jaguars were then vectored towards a barge in the Gulf, which they were cleared to engage. They were supported by a US Marine Corps A-6E Intruder, which marked the target for the Jaguars with its laser designator.

Between them, the Jaguars fired four pods of CRV7 rockets, but these all fell short of the target, so the pilots resorted to strafing the barge with 30 mm cannon. Despite firing 480 rounds of HE ammunition at it, the barge refused to sink. A second SUCAP pair was then tasked with attacking the barge, but they also proved unable to sink it. Meanwhile, a four-ship launched against artillery targets in the KTO had aborted its mission because of the deteriorating weather. It later transpired that the reason the SUCAP CRV7 rockets had missed their target was because the ballistics of an operational round were different to a training round, for which the weapon-aiming solution had been calculated.

On the morning of the following day (26 January), four Jaguars were tasked against a Hai Ying (HY-2) Silkworm SSM battery that had been

A close-up view of an AN/ALQ-101-10 EW pod on the port outer pylon of a Jaguar. The 'Dash Ten' pod was a deception jammer that manipulated and then re-transmitted radar signals to confuse the transmitting radar. It was effective against most Soviet-era AAA and missile radars (*Ian Black*)

set up on the coast just to the south of Kuwait City. The pilots easily found their target in excellent weather, but the bombing results were disappointing. Nos 1 and 3 missed entirely, and the bombs from No 4 caused only minor damage. However, No 2 scored direct hits with all four bombs.

A morning SUCAP armed with CRV7s was vectored onto a surface vessel, but it could not be positively identified as hostile because of smoke and oil on the water, so the aircraft did not engage it. That afternoon, five Jaguars attacked two M-46 artillery positions 30 miles south of Kuwait City, destroying one and damaging the other. The pilots also noted a third artillery position, which was reported back to the tasking agency.

Another mission against a Silkworm battery was carried out by four Jaguars on 27 January. The weather in the KTO was again poor, and an eight-ship that had launched earlier in the day had already been forced to abort the mission because of thick cloud up to 25,000 ft. Nevertheless, the lead pair of the second four-ship managed to locate the Silkworm battery and scored four direct hits on it. The second pair could not find the battery, so they bombed an ammunition storage site instead, which was their alternate target.

The weather had cleared the next day, and eight Jaguars attacked a barracks and an SSM site in the KTO. As with previous missions, the formation was sub-divided into two four-ships. The leading two aircraft bombed the SSM site successfully, but the Nos 3 and 4 found that the smoke from the leaders' bombs covered their aiming points, so they

Flg Off Malcolm Rainier, a pilot from No 54 Sqn, models the locally-produced 'desert' flying suit. The youngest Jaguar pilot to fly combat missions in Operation *Granby*, Rainier was awarded the DFC for his exploits during the conflict (*Malcolm Rainier*)

elected to bomb a D-30 battery which was deployed to the south of the barracks. All four aircraft in the second four-ship bombed the barracks, although once again an automatic weapons release malfunction caused one load to fall short.

The afternoon of 28 January also saw the first use of CBU-87 CBUs, which were employed against a large logistics site to the south of Kuwait City. 'As the conflict drew on', explained Flg Off Rainier, 'we rapidly exhausted ammunition and fusing options, so weapon-to-target matching became more or less irrelevant. Every target got a portion of Her Majesty's finest 1000-lb bombs. The lack of choice was exacerbated by our decision to drop slick munitions from on high.

'The BL755 anti-armour cluster munition was unable to function effectively from medium-level, so we needed an alternative. CBU-87 was swiftly cleared for use on the Jaguar, and we dropped it when tasked against area targets. The CBU-87 was marginally too long to be mounted on the tandem beam pylons, so we simply took one each on the inboard pylons. Unfortunately, the weapon aiming for the CBU-87 didn't arrive with it, which meant the early sorties used "reversionary" aiming. We had to achieve an exact dive angle and a specific speed for the required forward throw. Wind correction was non-existent.

'This was demanding stuff, and despite saying to ourselves that we would never re-attack, I found myself doing just that with a pair of these weapons, having failed dismally to meet the release criteria. I looked over my shoulder toward the target area, having pulled out of my first dive, and saw AAA shells detonating just below and behind my aircraft as I climbed for my second go. Re-attack was lunacy of course. Both engines in full reheat pointing toward the ground provided a lively heat source for any infra-red tracker or missile in southern Kuwait. Having been alerted to our presence by the lead pair, there were plenty of these.'

Nevertheless, despite the difficulties in using the new weapon, the first CBU-87 attack was a success, setting much of the target on fire. The two SUCAP missions flown that day were uneventful.

CBU-87 was also the weapon of choice for two missions mounted against Silkworm batteries in the KTO on 29 January. The weather was excellent, and two waves – an eight-ship (reduced to seven aircraft after a ground abort) in the morning and a five-ship in the afternoon – targeted the batteries located around the Iraqi naval facility at Ras al-Qulayah. Both missions were successful, and the second strike caused major damage to a radar site and support vehicles.

Whilst returning to Bahrain, the second formation observed four fast patrol boats (FPBs) heading southwards, and they reported their position to the Type 42 destroyer HMS *Gloucester*, which was on station in the area. As a result of this report, the two Jaguars on SUCAP duty were vectored to investigate the contacts. They discovered 16 FPBs, which 'greeted' them with accurate AAA fire. The FPBs were declared hostile, and each Jaguar made two weapon passes, firing all 76 CRV7 rockets. They hit at least one and possibly as many as four of the boats. A second pair of aircraft,

A Jaguar at low-level over the desert in full 'war fit' carrying four 1000-lb HE bombs, EW pods, self-defence AAMs and a centreline fuel tank. The 'false cockpit' painted in black on the nosewheel doors can be seen in this photograph (*Malcolm Rainier*)

being held at 30 minutes, readiness, was scrambled, and they too carried out a CRV7 attack on the FPBs, followed by a strafing pass. The surviving vessels were later engaged by Coalition naval helicopters, which claimed four FPBs sunk and the remainder damaged.

29 January was also notable for the first use of a new reconnaissance pod. A Vinten Vicon 18-603 Long Range Optical Pod (LOROP) had been loaned to the Jaguar detachment by the Army Air Corps at the start of hostilities. The pod, which had been previously mounted in a Beaver AL 1, offered an excellent stand-off capability thanks to its 36-inch lens, but work was needed to see if and how it could be integrated with the Jaguar. Sqn Ldr Dave Bagshaw, a very experienced fighter reconnaissance pilot, was given the task, and he carried out the first operational trial flight on the 29th;

'Flying above the expected AAA level, I slewed the LOROP camera to port, switched on, and flew a line search of the Kuwait and Saudi coasts until the film ran out. As I had learned from my colleagues' previous mission debriefs, the SkyGuardian RWR and audio "warble" in the earphones indicated some interesting threats, but with the ECM [electronic countermeasures] pod on "active" and loosing off some chaff, radar lock was broken, either by my own efforts or more likely by our *Wild Weasel* friends.

'The film was processed, but when viewed on the light table the PIs [Photographic Interpreters] began to scratch their heads. "Where's the coast 'Baggers'? Are you sure your eyesight is up to flying and navigating?" Following further learned cogitation, we twigged – looking at my map and comparing the film with terrain features to starboard of my track, we realised that LOROP had been pointing west instead of east – therefore, no coast!

'We re-consulted the sketchy bumph that had accompanied the kit and deduced that what we had thought was a rear view of the pod in the unannotated diagram was in fact a front view. So LOROP had been looking the wrong way! With left and right hand sorted, I flew trials on the following four days, again [with the jet] grafted onto a four-ship or a pair, flying at 25,000 ft and experimenting with differing angles of LOROP depression. On the fifth, and final, trip, my logbook records "mega cloud – acquisition by SA-2/SA-6 radars – overhead Kuwait International".

'When the results of the trials were assessed, the imagery indicated very high-definition cover of target areas from a stand-off distance of seven to eight kilometres at 25,000 ft, making it a really useful tool for pre-attack updates and, later, BDA [Bomb Damage Assessment].'

Tasking in the KTO switched from Silkworm batteries to artillery on 30 January. The first Jaguar mission of the day, involving eight aircraft, bombed two 2S1 Gvozdika 122 mm self-propelled gun batteries located about 20 miles southwest of Kuwait City. The aircraft were all loaded with CBU-87s. The formation leader later reported that the 'sortie [was] planned with four aircraft against each planned desired mean point of impact [DMPI]. Visibility was poor due to haze, with three- or four-eighths of cloud, with tops at 13,000 ft, which made target acquisition difficult. All aircraft dropped, less one hang-up which could not be released, on alternative target due to weather. No SAM or AAA seen.'

There was more action during the early afternoon SUCAP mission. After refuelling from a tanker, Wg Cdr Pixton and Flt Lt Pete Tholen were vectored to investigate a surface contact to the west of Faylaka Island. Once there, they discovered a Polnochny-class amphibious warfare ship. The Iraqi army had invaded Saudi Arabia during the previous night, and there was heavy fighting around the coastal town of Khafji – it seemed possible that this ship might be carrying reinforcements either towards Khafji or to Faylaka. After an initial pass to identify the vessel, the Jaguars obtained clearance to engage it, and they attacked using CRV7 and strafing.

'We released two pods of CRV7 each', recalled Tholen, 'aiming for the centre of the ship, which was approximately a pipper's width in depth. We attacked at a fairly shallow angle – partly due, weather constraints and partly due to the fact we believed the Polnochny had a reasonable defensive capability. It was also more akin to how we had flown strafe patterns. As we believed the vessel to be a valuable target, we then re-attacked it multiple times, which was against all our training!

'The weather on the day in question resulted in poor visibility, with a rather indistinct horizon. The pink Jaguar camouflage was very effective, and the other aircraft melted into the murk, so the Boss and I set up an academic pattern to strafe the boat with the HE 30 mm – we were calling "downwind", etc. to make sure we didn't end up with a mid-air! This we did for a few passes, aiming pretty much up and down the length of the vessel (until we ran out of ammo).'

While Pixton and Tholen engaged the Polnochny, five more Jaguars armed with CBU-87s headed for a command post in the KTO. Unfortunately, they found the target to be completely obscured by smoke, and they returned to Muharraq without dropping their weapons.

The tasking for the Jaguar detachment on 31 January followed the established pattern of a morning eight-ship and afternoon four-ship employed against targets in the KTO, plus two pairs for SUCAP missions. The morning target in the KTO was a large ammunition storage site and nearby logistics park located near the coast and close to the Ras al-Qulayah naval base. The formation leader elected to attack with a mix of weapons, and each of the constituent four-ships comprised one pair dropping four 1000-lb bombs and the other pair dropping two CBU-87s.

The first four-ship bombed the ammunition storage site, concentrating on the western part of the large-area target. The second

Cpl Chris Froome in front of Jaguar XZ119 *Katrina Jane* at Muharraq. The aircraft's artwork, painted by him, was based on photographs of his wife. Froome was responsible for much of the artwork that appeared on the Jaguars during the Gulf War (*RAF Museum*)

four-ship targeted the logistics park, but one Jaguar was locked up by the radar from a 'friendly' fighter and the pilot had to manoeuvre hard to break the lock. As a result, he was better placed to bomb the ammunition storage site.

Meanwhile, the SUCAP pair flown by Sqn Ldr Dick Midwinter and Flt Lt Simon Young had been re-tasked to carry out an armed reconnaissance of the main coastal highway in search of armoured vehicles travelling south. The Jaguars would be well placed to interdict any reinforcements heading to join the Battle of Khafji.

After the difficulties that had been encountered in aiming the CRV7 accurately, the weapon had been temporarily withdrawn and, on this day, the SUCAP Jaguars were each armed with four BL755 CBUs. Unfortunately, this weapon load restricted the aircraft to operating at low-level in an extremely high threat environment.

As they approached the highway, the pilots saw what they thought to be an armoured personnel carrier (APC) on the side of the road. Manoeuvring to attack it, they dropped their weapons onto the APC and a passing military lorry, destroying both. Midwinter was forced into a missile break as he came off the target in response to an SA-7 MANPADS launched against him, causing him to jettison his stores. It was only later that the APC was actually identified as a ZSU-23-4 'Shilka' self-propelled AAA gun – perhaps a lucky escape for the Jaguar pilots.

The afternoon wave of four CBU-87-armed Jaguars was tasked against another Silkworm battery at Ras al-Qulayah. They were joined by Sqn Ldr Dave Bagshaw with the LOROP, hoping to photograph the results of the strike so that proper BDA could be made and also detect the positions of other suitable targets for future attention. Although the formation did not encounter any defensive fire during their successful attack, they were constantly distracted by being locked up by 'friendly' fighters.

Fully armed with four 1000-lb HE bombs, Jaguar GR 1A XX962 is seen 'ready to go' at Muharraq. The tandem beam which enabled the inboard pylon to carry two bombs is clearly visible. Behind the aircraft are 2250-litre fuel tanks used by the Tornado GR 1s based at the airfield. XX962 completed 17 1000-lb HE bomb and 16 CBU-87 sorties during Operation *Granby* (*Michael Rondot*)

CHAPTER THREE

IRAQ – OPERATION *GRANBY*

1–28 February 1991

The target for the eight-ship of the day on 1 February was the support area at Ahmed al-Jaber air base, some 25 miles to the southwest of Kuwait City. One Jaguar suffered a ground abort when the NAVWASS failed, but the remaining seven aircraft, carrying a mix of 1000-lb freefall bombs and CBU-87s, found the target in excellent weather. Ahead of them, Kuwait Air Force A-4KU Skyhawks bombed the hangars to the north of the support area. The target itself was defended by light AAA that reached up to 15,000 ft.

Flying in the No 2 slot, Flt Lt Alex Emtage recalled that 'Once we dropped off the standard routing and entered the KTO, I selected min burner to gain altitude for the attack itself, with the aim being to enter the dive from as high an altitude as possible. Routing was effectively northbound, keeping Ahmed al-Jaber slightly to our right to give a right hand tip west-to-east attack run. To be honest, you could see the airfield from the border – great visibility and clear blue skies. The juicy [target] I had been given was the westerly hangar, just east of the runways, which I was delighted with and looked forward to hitting hard. Approaching the airfield, I continued until the hangar felt like it was by my right boot, then overbanked to the right to enter the dive and put the bomb fall line through the target.

XZ364 and XZ375, armed with CBU-87s, get airborne from Muharraq for a combat mission over Kuwait. Clearance to use this weapon came at the end of January 1991, and it proved ideal when attacking artillery targets. The 'Sadman' artwork and high number of mission markings painted on XZ364 date this photograph to the last days of Operation *Granby* (*Crown Copyright/MoD*)

'The attack was looking good – target bar stable on the centre of the hangar roof, with a solid laser ranging indication. I gently eased the dive to bring the release point forward and felt the bombs drop away in quick succession, the aircraft rocking as the release sequence was from alternate wings. Once I had recovered from the dive, I established a climb and, after about 30 seconds, dropped my right wing and looked over my shoulder to observe the fruits of my labour. To my huge disappointment (not quite how I voiced it at the time!) the impacts were very close, within ten metres as a guess, down the southerly side of the building, although the stick spacing was spot on, with all four bombs dropping along the length of the hangar.

'Wg Cdr Pixton once said that he could tell who had hit their respective targets by their faces when they walked into the Ops room back at Bahrain. Mine must have said it all. This was alleviated weeks later when the Boss showed me a post-conflict photograph of the hangar taken from the ground at Ahmed al-Jaber. The entire length of the building had been pushed in and the roof dropped.'

The two SUCAPs flown on that day had no trade, but a pair of Jaguars accompanied by the LOROP aircraft made a successful CBU-87 attack on the Ras al-Qulayah Silkworm site. On this sortie, the LOROP produced some excellent imagery, but it was still difficult to aim and as yet had proved to be of little use for BDA.

In contrast to the previous day, SUCAP Mission 4404A on 2 February was a busy one. After holding station near Faylaka Island until they reached fuel minima, the two Jaguars then refuelled. Shortly thereafter they were directed to call 'Berry 601', who tasked them with supporting a Combat Search And Rescue (CSAR) operation trying to locate a downed crew in the vicinity of Faylaka Island. Specifically, the Jaguars were to suppress the AAA defences on the island while a US Marine Corps A-6E Intruder made a low-level reconnaissance pass to search for survivors in the water. The pilots were warned to expect heavy AAA up to 12,000 ft and very heavy fire from small-calibre weapons up to 5000 ft.

After coordinating with the Intruder crew, the Jaguars ran across the island from north to south, delivering eight 1000-lb bombs onto AAA emplacements on concrete piers along the coast of the island. Once again, the pilots experienced difficulties with the automatic weapon release, and when the bombs did not drop automatically at 15,000 ft, they continued the dive and released them manually at 12,000 ft, scoring good hits on the AAA batteries. Meanwhile, the A-6E made its run and egressed safely from the area. Unfortunately, the next SUCAP sortie had to return to base when the leader suffered an engine surge after take-off.

Earlier that morning, eight Jaguars had carried out a strike on the Sabhan ammunition storage area next to Kuwait International Airport, south of Kuwait City, with CBU-87s. The formation encountered a heavy AAA barrage, causing one aircraft to miss the target as it was forced to manoeuvre to avoid the defensive fire. Heavy AAA also greeted a four-ship, accompanied by the LOROP aircraft, when they bombed the nearby Silkworm site in the afternoon with a mix of 1000-lb airburst bombs and CBU-87s. Marginal weather over the target, combined with the defensive fire and friendly aircraft in the same airspace, conspired to derail the attack.

In his mission report, the formation leader commented that 'F-16s in target area at [our] time over target caused loss of mission effectiveness. Marginal weather combined with friendly aircraft confliction in target area meant only one aircraft achieved the aim. All bombs not on DMPI fell in the sea'. The detachment commander added 'recce aircraft unable to gain useful photos. LOROP missions need further consideration before future tasking. Very heavy AAA [and] considerable friendly aircraft activity in the target area made the attack very difficult to complete'.

AIM-9L Sidewinder AAMs await loading onto Jaguars at Muharraq. Loading the missiles onto the overwing pylon of the Jaguar was a more complex procedure than, for example, the underwing location for the Tornado. The hoist needed to lift the missile above the wing can be seen here just ahead of the aircraft (*Malcolm Rainier*)

The Silkworm complex at Ras al-Qulayah was revisited the following day by two four-ships. The first four Jaguars dropped 12 airburst and four impact-fused 1000-lb bombs on the northerly-most battery, while the second four concentrated on the southerly battery, achieving good hits on the Type 347G ('Rice Bowl') fire control radar. The afternoon wave, flown once again as a five-ship with four bombers and the LOROP reconnaissance aircraft, targeted an artillery battery in the southern KTO. However, target acquisition was difficult, and although the leader dropped on the battery, the remaining three pilots attacked the Ras al-Qulayah Silkworm site instead.

Thick haze continued to make target acquisition difficult on 4 February, even against a large-area target, as two four-ships discovered that morning when they were tasked with attacking the barracks and extensive storage site to the north of Al Wafrah. Both formations made successful attacks (split by six minutes) on the same target, causing extensive damage to buildings and storage facilities. Haze made conditions challenging in the afternoon, too, when the four Jaguars of Mission 4411J rolled in on the command post of the Iraqi army's 3rd Corps, which was also north of Al Wafrah. However, the four-ship delivered its 1000-lb bomb loads accurately, despite AAA over the target and indications of a RPK-2 'Tobol' radar from a ZSU-23-4 'Shilka'.

The day also marked the last time that the Jaguars were tasked with SUCAP missions, enabling the flying programme to change to a morning and afternoon eight- or nine-ship on each day. These large formations were split into two four-ships, with varying differences in their times over the target so as to stay unpredictable to the defences. This new arrangement also enabled the detachment to formalise a five-day work pattern for the pilots within each constituted four-ship, consisting of four days of flying followed by a 'down day' to re-set.

On Day One (the first working day), the pilots flying the rear four aircraft of the afternoon eight-ship would then lead the afternoon eight-ship the following day. Day Three would see (*text continues on page 49*)

COLOUR PLATES

1
Jaguar GR 1A XX764/J of No 14 Sqn, Brüggen, West Germany, 1976

2
Jaguar GR 1A XX962/X (Operation *Granby*), JagDet Muharraq, Bahrain, January 1991

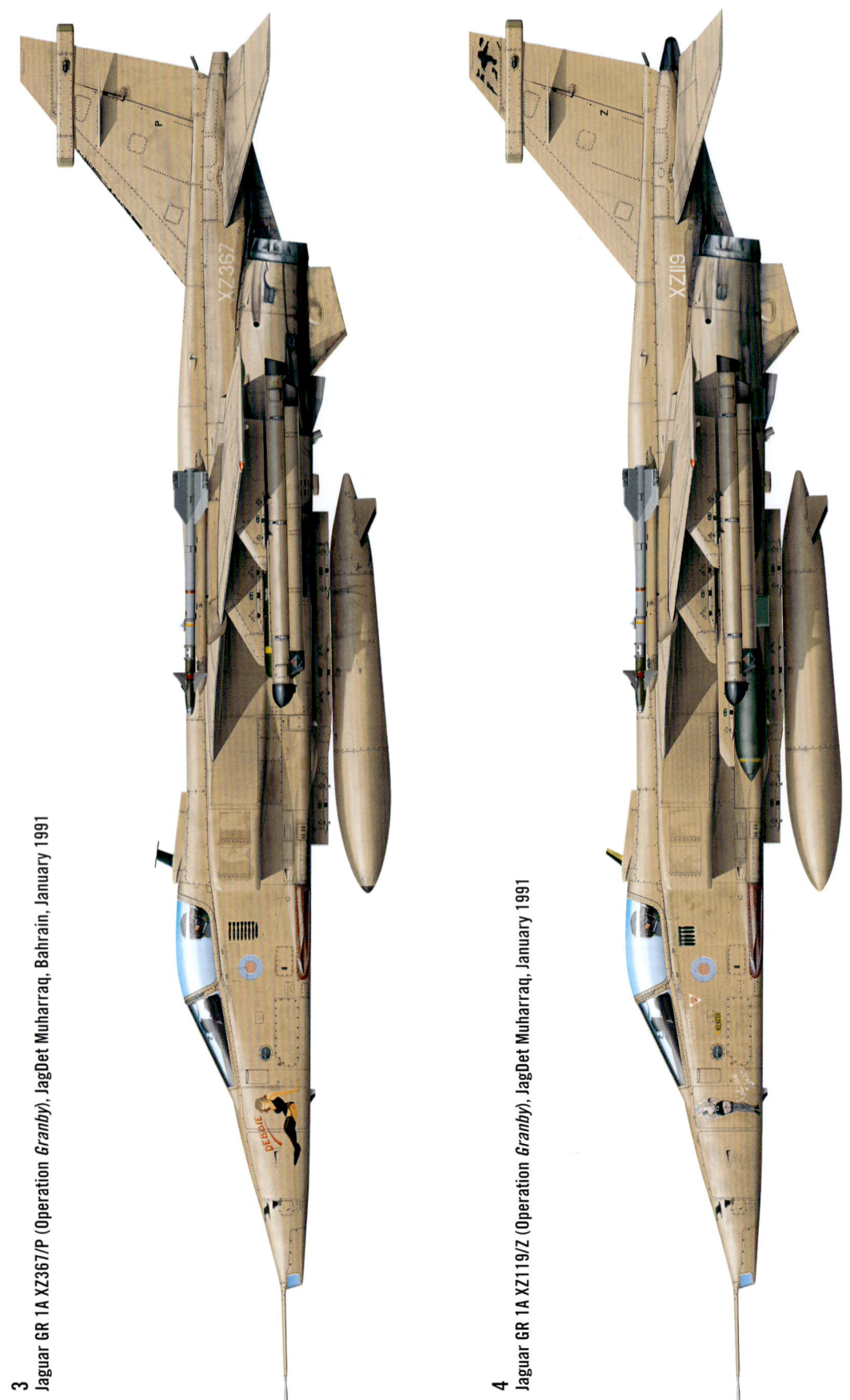

3
Jaguar GR 1A XZ367/P (Operation *Granby*), JagDet Muharraq, Bahrain, January 1991

4
Jaguar GR 1A XZ119/Z (Operation *Granby*), JagDet Muharraq, January 1991

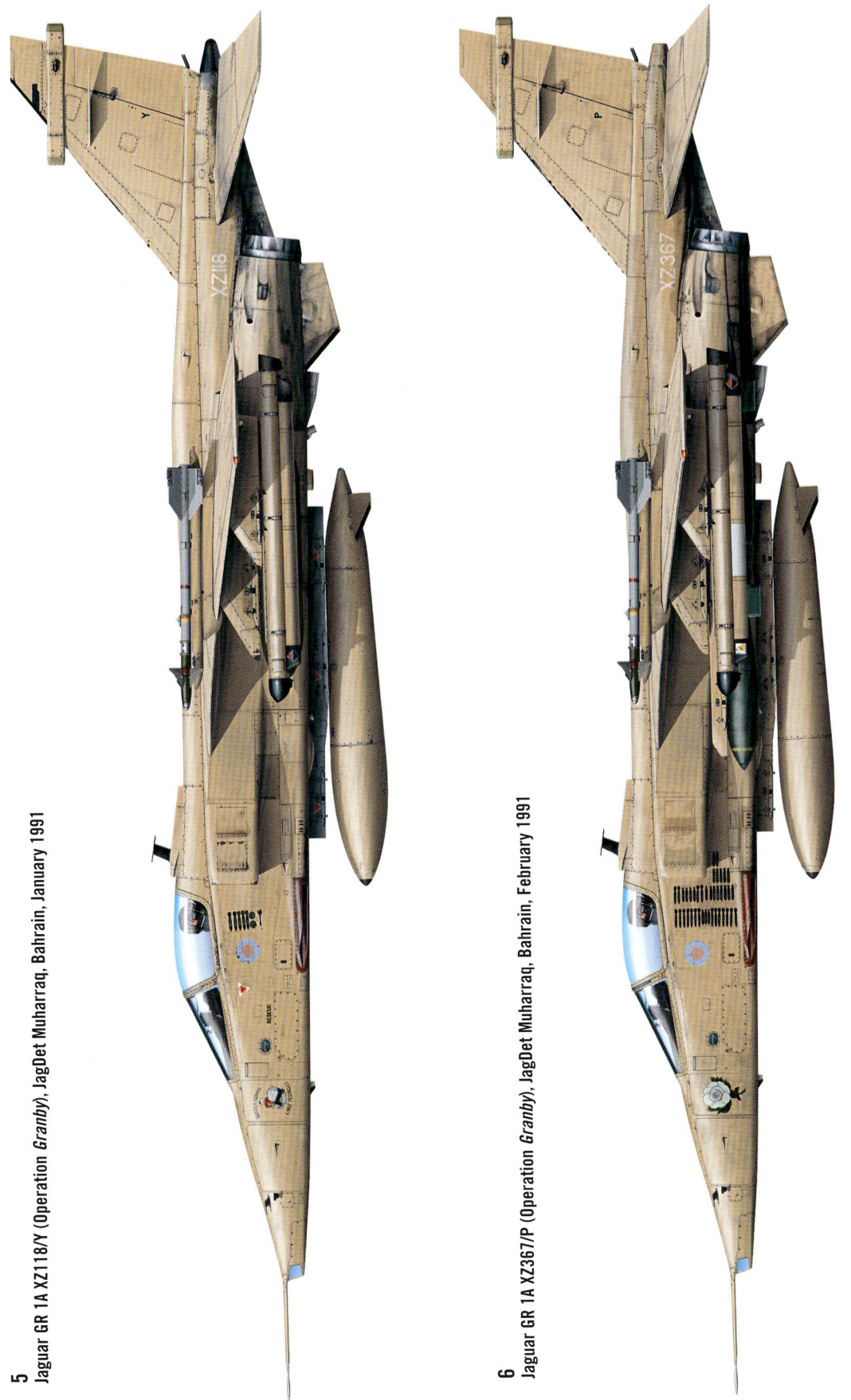

5
Jaguar GR 1A XZ118/Y (Operation *Granby*), JagDet Muharraq, Bahrain, January 1991

6
Jaguar GR 1A XZ367/P (Operation *Granby*), JagDet Muharraq, Bahrain, February 1991

7
Jaguar GR 1A XZ358/W (Operation *Granby*), JagDet Muharraq, Bahrain, February 1991

8
Jaguar GR 1A XX962/X (Operation *Granby*), JagDet Muharraq, Bahrain, February 1991

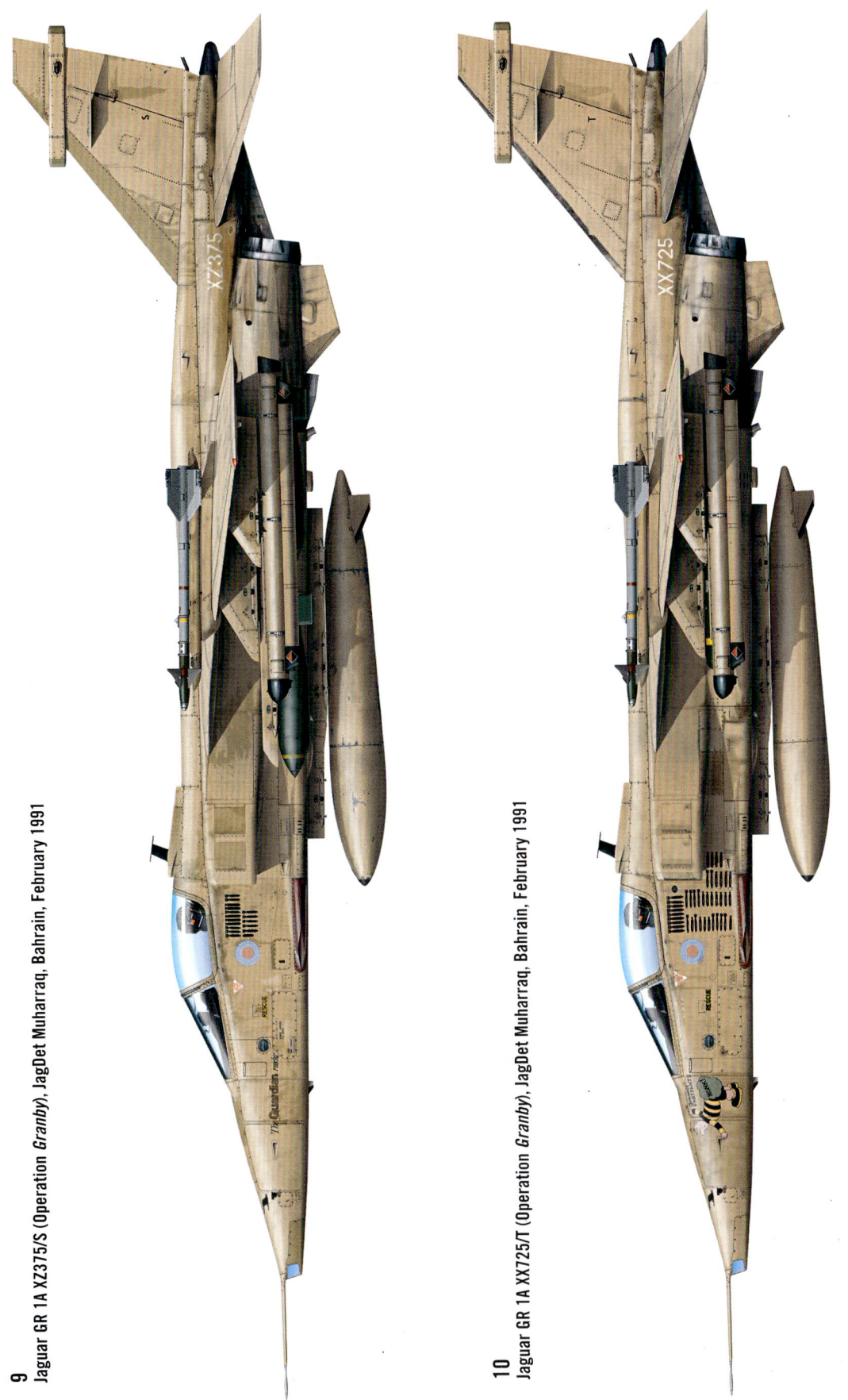

9
Jaguar GR 1A XZ375/S (Operation *Granby*), JagDet Muharraq, Bahrain, February 1991

10
Jaguar GR 1A XX725/T (Operation *Granby*), JagDet Muharraq, Bahrain, February 1991

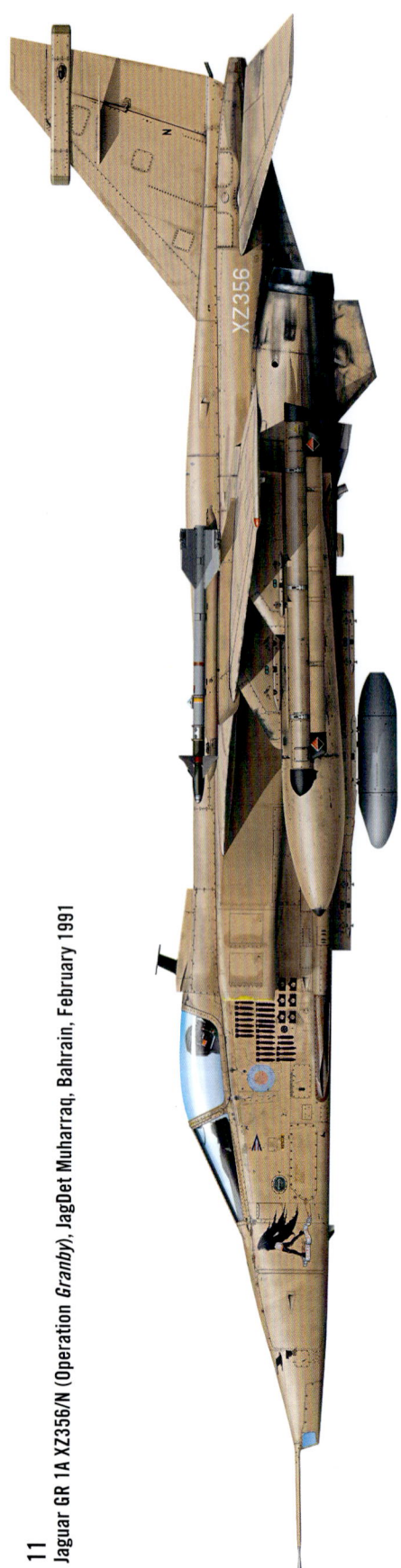

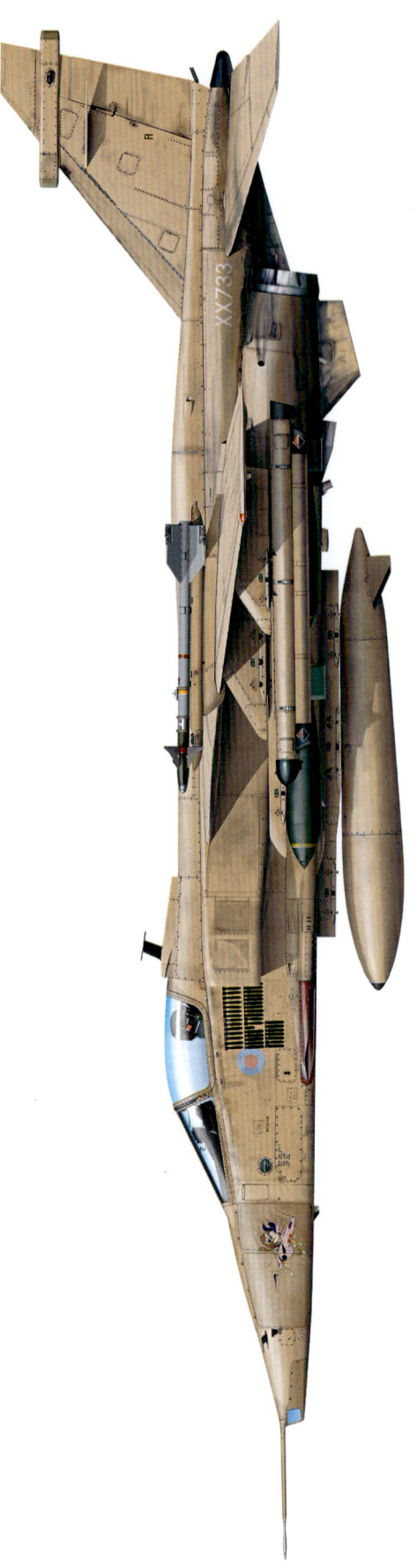

11
Jaguar GR 1A XZ356/N (Operation *Granby*), JagDet Muharraq, Bahrain, February 1991

12
Jaguar GR 1A XX733/R (Operation *Granby*), JagDet Muharraq, Bahrain, February 1991

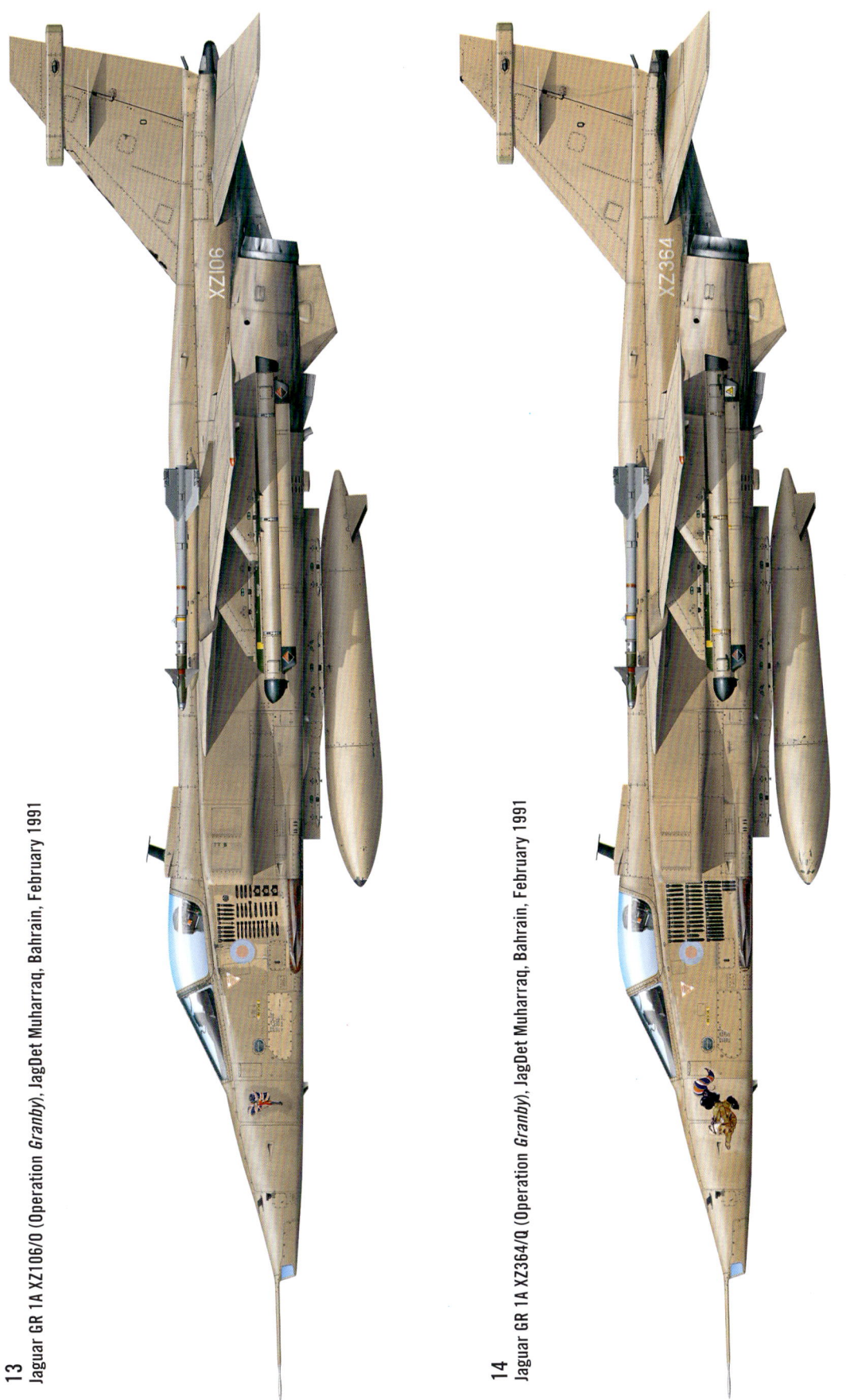

13
Jaguar GR 1A XZ106/0 (Operation *Granby*), JagDet Muharraq, Bahrain, February 1991

14
Jaguar GR 1A XZ364/Q (Operation *Granby*), JagDet Muharraq, Bahrain, February 1991

15
Jaguar GR 1A XZ114/FB (Operation *Warden*), Incirlik, Turkey, April 1993

16
Jaguar GR 1A XZ367/GP (Operation *Deny Flight*), Gioia Del Colle, Italy, November 1994

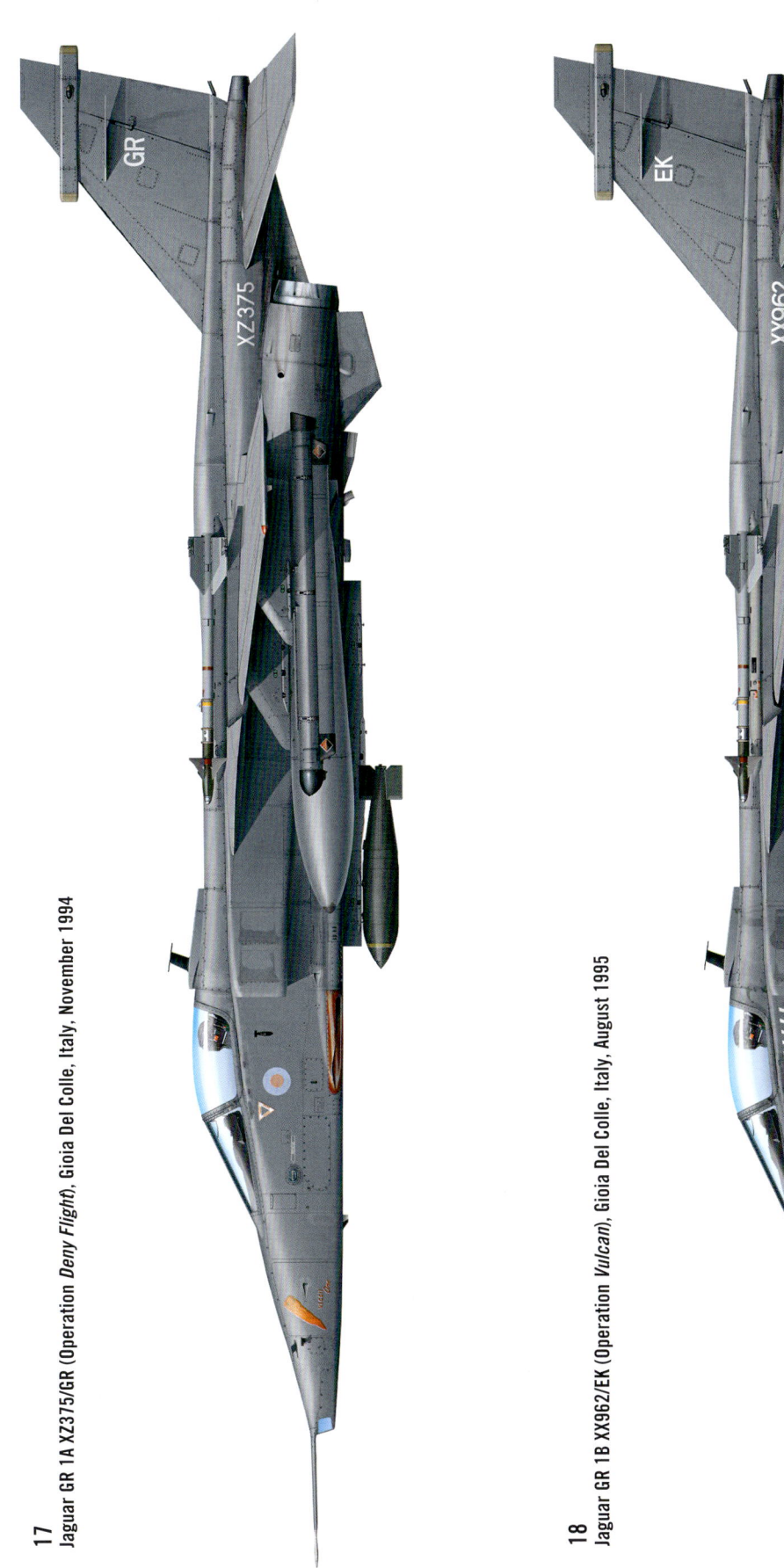

17
Jaguar GR 1A XZ375/GR (Operation *Deny Flight*), Gioia Del Colle, Italy, November 1994

18
Jaguar GR 1B XX962/EK (Operation *Vulcan*), Gioia Del Colle, Italy, August 1995

19
Jaguar GR 1B XX748/GK (Operation *Vulcan*), Gioia Del Colle, Italy, August 1995

20
Jaguar GR 3A XZ113/FD (Operation *Deliberate Guard*), Gioia Del Colle, Italy, July 1997

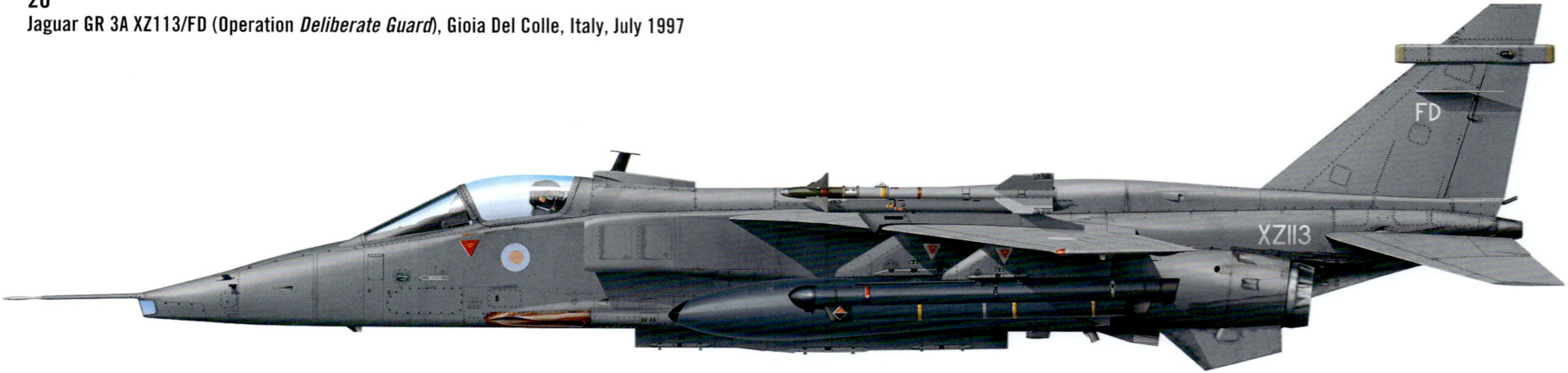

21
Jaguar GR 3A XZ357/FK of No 41 Sqn (Operation *Resinate North*), Incirlik, Turkey, February 1999

22
Jaguar GR 3A XX720/GB of No 54 Sqn (Operation *Resinate North*), Incirlik, Turkey, September 2002

1
Jaguar GR 1A XX764/J of No 14 Sqn,
Brüggen, West Germany, 1976

2
Jaguar GR 1A XX962/X (Operation *Granby*), JagDet
Muharraq, Bahrain, January 1991

3
Jaguar GR 1A XZ367/P (Operation *Granby*), JagDet
Muharraq, Bahrain, January 1991

4
Jaguar GR 1A XZ119/Z (Operation *Granby*),
JagDet Muharraq, January 1991

5
Jaguar GR 1A XZ118/Y (Operation *Granby*),
JagDet Muharraq, Bahrain, January 1991

6
Jaguar GR 1A XZ367/P
(Operation *Granby*), JagDet
Muharraq, Bahrain,
February 1991

7
Jaguar GR 1A XZ358/W (Operation *Granby*), JagDet Muharraq, Bahrain, February 1991

8
Jaguar GR 1A XX962/X (Operation *Granby*), JagDet Muharraq, Bahrain, February 1991

9
Jaguar GR 1A XZ375/S (Operation *Granby*), JagDet Muharraq, Bahrain, February 1991

10
Jaguar GR 1A XX725/T (Operation *Granby*), JagDet Muharraq, Bahrain, February 1991

11
Jaguar GR 1A XZ356/N (Operation *Granby*), JagDet Muharraq, Bahrain, February 1991

12
Jaguar GR 1A XX733/R (Operation *Granby*), JagDet Muharraq, Bahrain, February 1991

13
Jaguar GR 1A XZ106/O (Operation *Granby*), JagDet
Muharraq, Bahrain, February 1991

14
Jaguar GR 1A XZ364/Q (Operation *Granby*), JagDet
Muharraq, Bahrain, February 1991

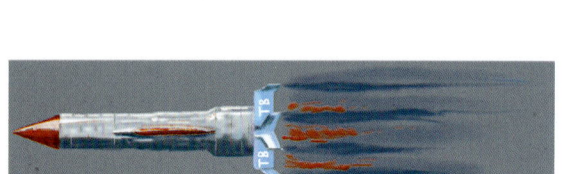

16
Jaguar GR 1A XZ367/GP (Operation *Deny Flight*),
Gioia Del Colle, Italy, November 1994

17
Jaguar GR 1A XZ375/GR (Operation *Deny Flight*),
Gioia Del Colle, Italy, November 1994

21
Jaguar GR 3A XZ357/FK of No 41 Sqn (Operation
Resinate North), Incirlik, Turkey, February 1999

22
Jaguar GR 3A XX720/GB of No 54 Sqn (Operation
Resinate North), Incirlik, Turkey, September 2002

them in the rear of the morning eight-ship, which they would lead on Day Four. Day Five was an opportunity to unwind and perhaps enjoy the delights of Bahrain.

The swift pace of operations was beginning to generate a problem with the rate at which the 1000-lb bombs and their fuses were being used up. Firstly, the limited stock of Mk 960 Multi-Function Bomb Fuses (MFBFs) was exhausted within the first few weeks, by which point most of the remaining allocation of Mk 947 tail fuses had been reserved for the Tornado forces' Laser-Guided Bomb (LGB) operations. Sqn Ldr Chris Allam recalled that 'we were therefore obliged to resort to using pistols and delayed arming devices and dispensed with fuses altogether. In the end, the shortage of 1000-lb bombs did not become critical, mainly due to the purchase of significant numbers of US-built cluster bomb units and, of course, the relatively short duration of the conflict'.

For Flg Off Malcolm Rainier, the abandoning of the MFBF 'may have had unintended benefits, as the second in my stick of two detonated at arming. Fortunately, we had set a sensible arming time, and I pulled out of the attack dive with considerable enthusiasm, giving plenty of sky between me and the bomb's fragments. A couple of Tornados were downed by this precise mechanism, and Thomson Thorn's assurances that fuse-at-arming was impossible turned out to be wide of the mark'.

The target for the morning nine-ship on 5 February was a radio relay station in the southern KTO. The two sub-formations attacked successfully with 1000-lb bombs 13 minutes apart. In the afternoon the eight-ship was tasked against an artillery battery, but neither of the constituent four-ships could find anything at the target coordinates. The lead pilot in the first four-ship dropped his weapons on a target of opportunity, but his wingmen brought their bombs back to Bahrain. In the second four-ship, following ten minutes later, all four pilots dropped on nearby AAA batteries in reveted positions after being unable to find the original target.

Tasking against artillery positions continued for the next three days, with variable results as cloud and haze made small targets such as artillery guns difficult to see. Sqn Ldr Allam later noted that 'as the conflict progressed, our tasking moved away from fixed installations and concentrated more on mobile artillery, self-propelled guns, towed artillery pieces and multi-barrel rocket launchers.

'This is where Air Headquarters taskers began to encounter problems – the Iraqis had prepared more positions in the desert than they had artillery pieces, and in some areas the desert was covered with sand revetments. Our taskers had problems identifying active positions and resorted to tasking us against targets "in the area of" a [grid reference]. This forced us into the armed reconnaissance role, which was less than ideal, although acceptable and still possible from high-level. These missions became known by the pilots as "spooning around in Kuwait".'

The weather improved on 9 February, enabling the nine aircraft in the morning wave to find their targets with relative ease. Four Jaguars were tasked against a logistics site, which they bombed with CBU-87s. Smoke made it difficult to determine how effective the attack had been, although the pilots were able to confirm that a scrapyard which had been fragged as their alternative target for the day was indeed full of military vehicles.

This information was passed on to the second formation of five Jaguars, which, following 13 minutes later, was intending to attack an artillery position with CBU-87s. Finding no artillery targets at the coordinates they had been given, the five aircraft bombed the scrapyard instead, causing severe damage there. The afternoon wave, which set out to bomb an MRL battery, was thwarted by clouds that had built up during the course of the morning. The first two aircraft managed to bomb the target, but of the next two Jaguars over the target, one had a weapons hang-up while the fourth elected to bomb a nearby Silkworm site which was active with support vehicles and possible missiles. The last four aircraft, who suffered communications jamming on their ingress, bombed an Iraqi command post instead.

Just three Jaguar four-ship missions were flown on 10 February. The first, which was reduced to three aircraft after a ground abort, was tasked against an artillery battery, but was given a late change of target coordinates. Good weather enabled the pilots to see that the new location was a 'target-rich environment', and they attacked an artillery concentration. The pilots also noted that there was a lot of smoke in the KTO, which was acting as a smoke screen and obscuring some of the target area.

The afternoon wave, consisting of two four-ships, attacked the Silkworm battery at Ras al-Qulayah, and thanks to clear weather, the pilots were able to acquire the target from 50 miles away. Flg Off Malcolm Rainier commented that 'the target sets became smaller and more mobile – artillery emplacements and suchlike, which were hard to find, or even entirely absent from the tasked coordinates. This necessitated the use of squadron recce assets to photograph the following day's target, using the cover of today's raid. The rear aircraft was mounted with a Vinten LOROP to achieve this'.

Clear weather on 11 February, as well as excellent photographs of the target – a Brazilian-manufactured Artillery SaTuration ROcket System (ASTROS) II MRL battery – helped the morning wave to achieve good hits on the launchers, as well as command and support vehicles. A second ASTROS II battery was to have been attacked by the afternoon wave, but the weather had deteriorated by then and all eight aircraft returned to base with their weapons.

An Iraqi army ASTROS II multiple rocket launcher battery in Kuwait. Rocket artillery batteries such as these were typical targets for the Jaguar detachment. The ASTROS II, which had a firing range of up to 25 miles, was sold to Iraq in numbers by the Brazilian company Avibras Aerospatial SA during the Iran–Iraq War of the 1980s (*US National Archive*)

From the end of January 1991, one aircraft equipped with an EMI Jaguar reconnaissance pod (seen here) and one with a LOROP accompanied attack missions over Kuwait to carry out post-strike reconnaissance for BDA and to identify new targets in the KTO. Following its retirement, Jaguar GR 1A XZ118 was displayed in the Tate Gallery in London in 2010–11, after which it was scrapped (*Michael Rondot*)

The day also saw the first mission (Mission 4411A) by a dedicated reconnaissance pair. 'A "recce pair" was constituted', recalled Sqn Ldr Dave Bagshaw. 'Myself, plus former "recce puke" Pete Livesey, flying one aircraft with LOROP and one with the F126 [reconnaissance pod]. The plan, as agreed with our man in Riyadh, was for us to be tasked as part of a Jaguar attack mission to provide post-attack BDA, as well as updated photos of targets to be tasked for the next day's missions.

'By leaving the cameras running as we departed the combat area, our PIs might also locate on film "targets of opportunity" which could be allocated to future missions. The recce pair first took to Kuwaiti skies on 11 February. There was thick cloud in the target area, but we filmed as much of the visible terrain as possible. Post-mission interpretation showed that the F126, when operated at 25,000ft, exposed the terrain at a scale very nearly that of the 1:50,000 maps used for target planning, whilst the LOROP produced excellent target detail, albeit covering a much smaller area.'

Missions against Iraqi MRL batteries continued into 12 February. The morning wave was met by an AAA barrage between 10,000–15,000 ft, although the first four aircraft were able to deliver their CBU-87s accurately onto the target. Five minutes later, the second four-ship armed with 1000-lb bombs had their attack run spoiled by two friendly fighters which appeared as the Jaguars were about to tip in over the target. The leader delayed his tip in, but could not then acquire the target, and instead bombed an AAA site. The other three aircraft carried out their attacks, but suffered some hang-ups and weapon-aiming problems that necessitated them jettisoning six bombs into the sea during the egress.

The afternoon wave had better luck, and despite another AAA barrage at 15,000 ft, the first pair dropped 1000-lb bombs onto the target, scoring good hits that were confirmed by the No 3 pilot. The latter elected to drop his CBU-87s onto an AAA site in the target area that was firing at the Jaguars, and his weapons caused a number of secondary explosions. The No 4 pilot dropped CBU-87s onto the MRL battery, causing a massive secondary explosion that could still be seen from 60 miles away during the recovery to base. As a result of these successes, the final four-ship found its target burning furiously, but nevertheless released its mixed load of 1000-lb bombs and CBU-87s onto the target area.

The reconnaissance pair covered an artillery position and a MRL battery. The artillery position was photographed by both the F126 and LOROP, confirming that the guns had moved to three new locations, coordinates for which were fed back to the tasking agency as targets for the next day's air strikes. Unfortunately, the LOROP missed the MRL battery, but there was sufficient coverage from the F126 pod to obtain accurate coordinates for the weapon system.

The morning wave on 13 February was split in order to attack two different targets – one four-ship, armed with 1000-lb bombs, focused on a communications post near to Kuwait International Airport, while the second four-ship bombed an artillery battery with a mixed load of 1000-lb bombs (dropped by the first pair) and CBU-87s (dropped by the second). The communications post proved to be difficult to locate precisely, and clouds in the area as well as frequent lock-ups by SA-2 radars added to the task. Despite these challenges, all 16 bombs were delivered onto the target.

Further to the south in the KTO, the weather was still clear, so the Jaguars tasked against the artillery battery were able to find their target easily. The weather remained clear in the afternoon, and both four-ships in the second wave also had no problems finding their targets – an artillery battery and a MRL battery. The pilots were helped by the photographs taken by the reconnaissance pair on the previous day. Both formations were also fired on by AAA as they crossed the coast into the KTO, and heavy AAA and an SA-16 MANPADS was fired at them in the target area. The reconnaissance pair also launched in the afternoon, but the F126 pod

Another groundcrew nose art artist was Cpl Paul Robins, seen here in front of his 'pink Spitfire' artwork on Jaguar XX733. The cartoon pilot was based on Sqn Ldr Dave 'Baggers' Bagshaw, who had flown his 4000th Jaguar flying hour on a sortie during the lead-up to Operation *Granby*, and who flew many of the reconnaissance missions undertaken by the JagDet during the conflict (*RAF Museum*)

Flt Lt Nick Collins, Flg Off Malcolm Rainier and Flt Lt Dave Foote were amongst the junior pilots in the Jaguar detachment at Bahrain during Operation *Granby*. Next to them, a weapon load team are arming an aircraft with 1000-lb HE bombs in readiness for its next mission (*Malcolm Rainier*)

failed and continuing problems with the LOROP meant that the mission was not a success.

By now a heavy AAA barrage was a feature of most missions over the KTO at around 15,000 ft, and at this height it unfortunately coincided with the weapon release altitude during the 30-degree dive profile. Sqn Ldr Bagshaw described how 'during the early missions, the 30-degree dive profiles placed the aircraft well within the AAA lethal envelope during recovery after weapon release, as evidenced by shell bursts seen above the "bottom out" altitude. Fortunately, little damage was suffered by aircraft or pilots, but a lump of spent shrapnel dented the underside of the boss's aircraft pretty much in line with the base of the ejection seat!

'To lessen the risk, steeper dive angles would ensure a higher recovery height after bomb release, and also potentially offer better accuracy. The QWIs suggested 45 degrees – then 60 degrees – and went off to crunch the numbers to come up with the correct depression and required HUD sight picture. In order to achieve a stabilised 60-degree dive with the HUD "bomb fall line" tracking the target, it was necessary to tip in from the highest possible altitude. The technique was to select part throttle reheat approaching the Initial Point [IP] and maintain a gentle climb until target acquisition. I can vividly recall seeing 32,000 ft in the HUD as I rolled (gently, gently) over into the dive!'

Sqn Ldr Chris Allam confirmed that 'in later attacks we were tipping in from about 32,000 ft into a 35–60-degree dive and releasing at about 20,000 ft', but as Flg Off Malcolm Rainier pointed out, 'we had to watch the Mach up there, because we needed to release while still subsonic, and the jet accelerated briskly in the dive'.

The higher angle dive profile was used to good effect for the first time on 14 February. The morning wave achieved good hits with CBU-87s on an artillery battery, including the destruction of the battery command post behind the gun line. The leader of the second four-ship reported 'a very successful sortie flown in good weather. This sortie proved the value of good intelligence, and increasing familiarity with aiming the CBU-87 showed that results are rapidly improving. Best sortie for this constituted four-ship so far'. The afternoon eight-ship also enjoyed success against a D-20 152 mm towed howitzer battery. Good weather allowed the reconnaissance pair, carrying two serviceable pods, to locate and photograph an artillery battery and an ASTROS II MRL battery.

The imagery collected proved most valuable the next morning when two four-ships attacked the ASTROS II battery. Working with good target photographs in excellent weather, the first four-ship delivered its CBU-87s and achieved good hits that were confirmed by the second formation, which reported seeing command and control elements and several vehicles burning. This second four-ship found its attack complicated by three F-16s attacking the same target at the same time, but the Jaguar pilots nevertheless managed to hit their DMPIs.

In the afternoon, the efforts of both four-ships were directed against a 2S1 self-propelled gun battery, but they found that the target had already been decimated shortly beforehand by an F/A-18 mission. However, a few guns still appeared to be intact, so the first four Jaguars released their weapons onto the site to mop up any remaining artillery pieces. The pilots in the second four-ship decided to attack several other artillery emplacements nearby in what they described as a 'target rich environment'. The reconnaissance pair also achieved good results on their sortie.

The Iraqi army had started to set oil wells alight in the south of the KTO, and by 16 February the whole of southern Kuwait was blanketed by a thick layer of black smoke. The morning wave found target acquisition against artillery positions impossible in these conditions, and all eight aircraft returned to Bahrain with their weapons on board. As a result, the afternoon wave was allocated its target – a M-46 130 mm towed field gun battery – in the clearer area further to the north. Both four-ships located the target and attacked it successfully with CBU-87s despite heavy AAA fire in layers between 8000–10,000 ft and again at 15,000 ft. The second four-ship reported that 'a total of eight CBU-87s released onto the target, but BDA was impossible as the formation was more interested in running away bravely from all the AAA'. Smoke and poor weather combined the next day to make conditions unsuitable for air operations over the KTO and flying was cancelled.

Smoke continued to be a factor over the next few days, and all the Jaguar attack missions flown on 18 February saw pilots drop their weapons on a large logistics site, rather than on their tasked targets which were hidden under the smoke. The reconnaissance pair was more flexible, however, and pushed further north to get some photographic area coverage for the US Marine Corps.

On 19 February the smoke had abated enough to consider launching the Jaguars against artillery targets once more. The first four-ship of the day located an M-46 battery and pressed home its attack despite the fact that there was still some dense smoke in the area. Each pilot was able to select an individual gun in one of the many reveted positions to target with their CBU-87s. During this attack an aircraft was locked up by an SA-6 system, but the pilot managed to break the lock.

The second four-ship was informed as they transited towards the KTO that their prime and back-up targets, both artillery, were obscured by smoke, and they were re-tasked against artillery scrapes under clearer airspace. This attack was also successful, and the afternoon wave had a very similar experience. The reconnaissance pair covered several targets in the KTO, reporting that 'while filming, the pair encountered heavy AAA both at 12,000 ft, well below them, and at 22,000 ft, not so well below them, and managed to locate a 100 mm AAA site as it fired'. After covering their targets, the two aircraft carried out a complete sweep of the Kuwait–Saudi border at the request of Army planning staff.

Alternate targets were the flavour of the day on 20 February, too. The first four-ship into the KTO bombed a logistics site in poor weather, and the second four-ship also attacked its alternative target (an artillery position). One afternoon formation, reduced to a pair because of serviceability issues, made a successful attack on an MRL battery, which was located easily thanks to excellent imagery taken by the reconnaissance pair on a previous day. However, the second formation following shortly afterwards found the battery was now under partial cloud cover at 5000 ft. Although three aircraft were able to drop their weapons, one pilot was unable to identify the target and brought his ordnance back to base.

In a busy sortie that day, the reconnaissance pair covered 19 different oil distribution points that had controlled fire trenches along the Kuwaiti and Iraqi borders with Saudi Arabia in order to confirm BDA after F-117s had carried out attacks on them.

Both of the morning four-ships on 21 February brought their weapons home, having not dropped because of extensive cloud in the KTO, but much of that had cleared by the afternoon when two four-ships were tasked against an MRL battery. It was located despite thick oil smoke and some lingering cloud thanks to the photographs taken previously by the reconnaissance pair. The weather conditions made it difficult to pick out individual targets, so the CBU-87s were dropped into the target area, which was known to be full of artillery. Smoke also affected the activities of the reconnaissance pair, who found some of their tasked targets, but then moved southwards into clearer air to photograph the border defences on the Kuwait–Saudi border for use by the Joint Force Headquarters planning staff.

Visibility was even worse the next day, when a temperature inversion at 9000 ft held down all of the smoke and dust, and once again the morning wave did not drop their weapons because of the difficulties in target acquisition. The afternoon targets were further to the north where the

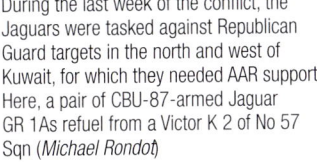

During the last week of the conflict, the Jaguars were tasked against Republican Guard targets in the north and west of Kuwait, for which they needed AAR support. Here, a pair of CBU-87-armed Jaguar GR 1As refuel from a Victor K 2 of No 57 Sqn (*Michael Rondot*)

air was clearer, making it much easier to locate the target (an artillery battery deployed in revetments) for the first four-ship. After the attack, as the formation was egressing, the leader saw an SA-2 SAM fired from short-range ahead of him, but the missile was unguided and he was able to avoid it. The second four-ship attacked an MRL battery, causing secondary explosions on the ground.

Having spent much of the previous four weeks operating in the southern part of the KTO between Kuwait City and Al Wafrah, the Jaguar detachment began to be tasked against targets further to the north and west, where the visibility was better. These longer-range attacks required AAR support.

On 23 February the target was an Iraqi Republican Guard artillery battery that was deployed in the far west of Kuwait, close to the Iraqi border. The morning wave was split into two four-ships, with time over target being 30 minutes apart. This would give both formations plenty of time for refuelling, and also allow the second four-ship to catch the target defences off guard. After refuelling, the first four-ship found its target easily, but also discovered that it was already under attack by RSAF F-5E Tiger IIs. The leader elected to switch to the alternative target (another gun line), which they bombed with 1000-lb bombs. Thirty minutes later, the second four-ship found that they were following three B-52 Stratofortresses through the target area. Although the USAF bombers were described by the formation leader as 'an awesome sight', it forced the pilots to switch to their alternate target. Meanwhile, the reconnaissance pair flew their daily sortie in the morning.

On the same day, having previously been temporarily withdrawn from service a few weeks beforehand, the CRV7 rocket reappeared in the inventory, with a new software programme for the weapon-aiming system. The rockets were loaded to the Nos 3 and 4 aircraft in the first formation of the afternoon, with the leader and No 2 aircraft carrying CBU-87s. The formation carried out a successful attack against an artillery field gun battery, reporting 'first use of CRV7 new software very successful. All rockets hit selected target and white smoke seen from target post impact.' A second four-ship following 15 minutes later was tasked against the same Republican Guard artillery as the morning wave, and without the distraction of F-5s or B-52s in the area, the pilots were able to drop their CBU-87s onto a Vee-shaped artillery position.

One of the biggest challenges faced by the Jaguar detachment in Bahrain as the conflict progressed was the lack of enough bomb fuses. The 1000-lb HE weapons on this aircraft are armed with VT (airburst) fuses which can be seen on the nose of the bomb visible in the photograph. During the final stages of Operation *Granby*, the detachment had to rely on World War 2-vintage pistol fuses. XX725 dropped 1000-lb HE bombs on 21 sorties and CBU-87s on 20 sorties (*Michael Rondot*)

The ground campaign commenced in the early hours of 24 February when Coalition forces advanced into Kuwait and Iraq. For the Jaguar detachment, the targets were again Republican Guard artillery batteries in western Kuwait, which meant AAR was required to reach them. Unfortunately, poor weather caused the first four-ship problems in rendezvousing with its tanker, and when the aircraft was eventually found, refuelling had to take place at the relatively low level of 4000 ft.

The lead Jaguar then experienced a burst refuelling hose, which caused fuel to go down both engine intakes, filling the cockpit with acrid blue smoke. The leader therefore returned to base, leaving the others to refuel on the single remaining hose. Unfortunately, this took longer than originally planned (based on two hoses being available), and the No 3 pilot could not make his designated time over target so, like the leader, he had to abort. The other two pilots carried out their CBU-87 attacks successfully.

Following just five minutes later, a second Jaguar four-ship was armed with CRV7 rockets. They also completed their refuelling in challenging conditions but found their target in clear weather. Problems using frequency-agile radios to communicate with the US Marine Corps control agencies meant that clearance to fire the weapons was not obtained until just two minutes from the target. Nevertheless, the attacks were successful, and all pilots scored direct hits with their rockets. The reconnaissance pair ventured into Iraq itself and obtained some excellent images with the LOROP, despite almost continuous lock-ups by SA-2, SA-6 and SA-8 radars.

Later in the day, the frontlines had moved sufficiently that the Republican Guard artillery targets for the first afternoon four-ship were too close to friendly forces for the Jaguars to attack them. The formation was sent to another artillery target five miles further north, which it attacked with CRV7s. Thirty minutes later, the weather on the refuelling tracks had deteriorated further, and two Jaguars in the second four-ship had to divert to the airfield at Al Jubail, in Saudi Arabia, when they could not find their tanker. The other pair in the formation had more luck with the refuelling, but could not then obtain clearance from the control agency to release their weapons, so they too were forced to abort the mission.

All four of the four-ship attack missions tasked into the KTO on 25 February encountered bad weather over the target areas and had to abort without releasing their weapons. The reconnaissance pair was also unable to take any imagery because of the weather over Kuwait. The pattern was repeated on the 26th, although the reconnaissance pair did fly again, only to be thwarted by clouds.

'Our final mission on 27 February suffered the same fate', wrote Sqn Ldr Bagshaw, 'but recce results were not completely zero. As we were walking out [to the aircraft], one of the PIs intercepted us. "Hey, 'Baggers', HQ staff want to know if the Kuwait City water towers are still standing. Can you have a look?" "Okay", I replied, "if the fuel holds out". Our planned route took us near the city, so as we approached, I told 'Livo' that I was about to take the plunge, and that he was welcome to stay above cloud and head on home. He wisely decided to take no part in this madness, so I rolled into the dive and pressed on down through 20,000 ft of grotty cloud. I broke out at 2500 ft just east of the city centre. The towers were still standing and apparently intact, so I rolled belly-up to point my F126 and F95 vertical cameras in their general direction. Just in case any trigger-happy bad (or good) guys might take a final pot shot, I effected a rapid recovery back into the murk, climbed back on top and made an uneventful recovery to Muharraq'.

The missions undertaken on 27 February turned out to be the last ones flown by the Jaguars during Operation *Granby*. With hostilities over, the aircraft, pilots and groundcrew returned to Coltishall in the second week of March. In retrospect, the participation in the conflict by the RAF Jaguar force was summed up eloquently by Sqn Ldr Chris Allam;

'I suppose that the overall results speak for themselves. Iraqi forces left Kuwait six weeks after the beginning of the Coalition air campaign and 96 hours after the start of the ground offensive. Although detailed BDA was difficult to acquire at squadron level, especially during the conflict, post-conflict analysis of our targets would suggest that a lot of them had been more heavily damaged than we might have first thought. Similarly, I like to think that the speed of advance through the KTO and the small number of casualties incurred by Coalition ground forces was due, in at least some part, to the effectiveness of the Jaguars.

'In terms of statistics, the Jaguars flew 618 sorties during the six-week period of the air campaign, with only seven sorties classified as "duty not carried out" due to aircraft serviceability. The breakdown, by mission type, was 72 per cent interdiction, 15 per cent SUCAP/CSAR and 13 per cent reconnaissance. Electing to operate at high-level, despite the problems that this generated, was the best and most important decision we made throughout the conflict. Had we fought the way we had trained, at low-level in daylight, it is unlikely that all 22 pilots would have come home. However, even though we didn't use our low-level skills, our familiarity with high workload situations that we had gained by training at low-level stood us in good stead for the increased pressures of the conflict.'

A post-war photograph of representatives of all the RAF tactical aircraft types which participated in Operation *Granby*. Led by Jaguar GR 1A XZ367 are a Tornado F 3, a Buccaneer and a Tornado GR 1. All of the aircraft are loaded with typical war loads and role equipment from the conflict (*Ian Black*)

CHAPTER FOUR

NORTHERN IRAQ – OPERATION *WARDEN/RESINATE*

September 1991 – February 2003

Flt Lt Andy Cubin prepares to climb aboard his Jaguar at Incirlik for a mission in the NFZ over northern Iraq. The aircraft is painted in the 'desert pink' ARTF camouflage of the Gulf War, and it is in the same configuration that was used by the JagDet for reconnaissance sorties during the conflict. The GA code on the nosewheel door indicates that the Jaguar belongs to No 54 Sqn (*Andy Cubin*)

Shortly after the Iraqi army had been defeated in Kuwait, there was an uprising in March 1991 by the ethnic Kurdish population of northern Iraq against the government of President Saddam Hussein. Unfortunately for the Kurds, the Iraqi army was not completely broken, and its troops swiftly and brutally quashed the insurrection. As a result, many Kurds fled to Turkey and Iran, but others were left homeless, leading to a humanitarian crisis in northern Iraq.

US and Coalition governments provided humanitarian aid to these refugees, and also gave them military protection, part of which was the establishment of a No-Fly Zone (NFZ), preventing Iraqi forces from operating aircraft north of the 36th Parallel. The British contribution to the enforcement of the NFZ comprised eight Jaguars from No 54 Sqn, which were deployed to Incirlik, in Turkey, on 4 September 1991. The Jaguars were supported by two Victor tankers based at Akrotiri. Within 36 hours of their arrival at Incirlik, the Jaguars had flown their first missions and delivered the first imagery.

Enforcement of the NFZ was codenamed Operation *Northern Watch* by the Americans and Operation *Warden* by the British. The Right Honourable Tom King, Secretary of State for Defence, declared that 'our aircraft are deploying to Turkey to join US and French aircraft as part of the contribution we have been making to the continuing presence in the area. The purpose of these deployments is to provide reassurance to the people of northern Iraq and maintain the Coalition's capability to respond swiftly and effectively to any Iraqi behaviour which might threaten local peace and security'.

The primary mission of the Jaguars in Operation *Warden* was tactical reconnaissance and the surveillance of Iraqi ground forces. The US military had moved away from using aircraft as tactical reconnaissance platforms, relying instead on satellites. These were ideal for the strategic task, but their relatively slow response time made them unsuited for tactical work, thus causing a capability gap at the tactical level. Carrying the EMI reconnaissance pod, the Jaguars could easily fill this gap, and provide commanders with photographic imagery of a point of interest within a few hours of being tasked for the mission.

Paradoxically, while the Jaguar detachment that had flown in the attack role during the Gulf War had been commanded by Wg Cdr William Pixton, a reconnaissance specialist, the new reconnaissance detachment would be led initially by Wg Cdr Tim Hewlett commanding No 54 Sqn, an attack unit. The team selected by Hewlett for the first deployment to Turkey included some very experienced pilots. 'I first deployed to Incirlik as operations commenced in September 1991', recalled Flt Lt Andy Cubin. 'This was my fourth consecutive Jaguar tour, and I was an eight-ship leader and one of the most experienced Jaguar pilots on the squadron.

Flt Lt Andy Cubin finds an Iraqi MiG-23 'Flogger' at Tal Afar air base, some 40 miles west of Mosul. He later recalled 'I ran towards the open door of the HAS, cameras running. There in front of me, just being towed out of the HAS, was an MiG-23 "Flogger" – I had to ease up slightly as I went past, and recall seeing one Iraqi soldier duck with his hands on his ears' *(Andy Cubin)*

My first tour, some six years previously, was as a reconnaissance specialist on No 41 Sqn. This recce experience would stand me in good stead for the current op'.

Daily tasking into the NFZ normally called for three pairs of Jaguars launching in sequence to cover an extended time window over northern Iraq. The tasking would be promulgated on the previous day, specifying between six and ten reconnaissance targets. Some of the targets were static, such as Republican Guard headquarters, Iraqi army barracks and equipment, or the air base at Tal Afar, to the west of Mosul. This latter airfield was a regular target since its HASs had not been damaged during the Gulf conflict and were being used to shelter MiG-23 fighters.

Missions tasked with covering static targets were relatively straightforward to plan, but many of the targets were mobile, and in those cases the pilots relied on the results of previous reconnaissance sorties, or recent US satellite imagery, for planning. The mobile targets were generally tasked as a line search, which in Sqn Ldr Cubin's opinion 'was more difficult as the pilot would need to follow a road or railway line and then visually identify and film targets as they appeared on the search – not easy at 450 knots'.

The Jaguar reconnaissance pod used wet film and was designed for the low-level role. 'Even if the pilot could not visually identify a target', explained Cubin, 'if he flew the aircraft over or near the coordinates whilst filming, the target would be on the film somewhere. Aiming a specific outer camera took a bit of practice – the canopy inline paint mark made for a good aiming tool. Run that mark through the bottom of the target and the resulting image would be centred on the negative. The 30 per cent overlap [of images] meant that, on the photographic light table, the PI would be able to analyse the image in 3D when viewed through a stereoscope'. On occasions a LOROP would be carried instead of the Jaguar reconnaissance pod, enabling the pilots to take high-resolution imagery of Iraqi military targets south of the 36th parallel.

A typical Operation *Warden* sortie would consist of an hour-long transit to the entry point into Iraqi airspace, accompanied by a tanker. The Jaguars were configured with either a reconnaissance pod or 1000-lb bombs depending on the mission requirements, an AN/ALQ-101-10 pod and Phimat chaff dispenser. They were also armed with overwing AIM-9L Sidewinder AAMs and two 30 mm cannon, each loaded with 120 rounds of HE ammunition, for self-defence. During the period that aircraft were operating in the NFZ, USAF fighters (F-15s or F-16s), supported by an E-3A Sentry Airborne Warning And Control System (AWACS) aircraft, ensured that Iraqi fighters did not interfere with Coalition reconnaissance assets. The USAF also provided *Wild Weasel* SEAD and CSAR support, the latter by helicopters escorted by A-10s.

Wg Cdr Hewlett recalled that 'initially, there were multiple challenges. Our tankers were based in Cyprus and had to get airborne and clear of Greek airspace to meet us over Turkey, flying parallel to the Syrian/Turkish border as we headed eastwards. Our AAR area was over high ground, generating unwelcome turbulence and cloud. The aircraft were fully laden with reconnaissance cameras, ECM pods, fuel tanks and AIM-9 Sidewinder missiles mounted on overwing stations which compounded handling difficulties behind the tanker and when plugged in. Refuelling was quite hazardous, and those who had not done much before found it difficult'.

The Victors were redeployed from Akrotiri to Incirlik in early 1992, which greatly simplified the organisation of Jaguar sorties. Initially, it was thought that two Jaguars would have to be sacrificed to make space for the tankers, but the Turkish authorities permitted the force level to remain at eight Jaguars. The Victors were replaced by VC10K tankers later in the year.

Sqn Ldr Cubin described a typical Operation *Warden* mission from the pilot's perspective;

'My day would start at 0330 hrs. I liked the dawn patrol for two good reasons. First, the average Iraqi would not be pointing his weapon skyward at me just as the sun was coming up because he'd still be rubbing the sleep from his eyes. Second, once the mission photographs had been analysed by the PIs, I'd be finished for the day and it would still only be 1030 hrs – a good time to hit the pool, drive out sightseeing in Turkey or bash the skin off a golf ball on the air base's very own nine-hole golf course.

'The first wave, with an airborne time of 0500 hrs, would drive from the Officers' Quarters to the Pilot's Briefing Facility [PBF] by minibus. The PBF, by the time the pilots arrived, was a buzz of activity. Weather brief, intelligence brief and final planning refinements done, the pilots would sanitise and don their war kit. Name and squadron badges, normally affixed to the pilot's overalls by Velcro, would be detached and left in the pilot's cupboard. All personal effects also remained behind, to be replaced by a strip of gold sovereigns, a Goolie Chit [a piece of paper on which details written in Arabic, Farsi and other local dialects promised great rewards if the pilot was returned in one piece!] and a fully loaded Walther PPK. All this kit added about ten kilogrammes to the pilot's normal weight, which had to be taken into account when dialling-in the mass on the ejector seat rocket pack adjuster.

'We were ready for war. Normally, there was a four-ship on the first wave. The joking would finish as we mounted the minibus again, to be driven to the HAS site were the jets were being prepped by the early groundcrew shift. The pilots would usually be quietly contemplative. Despite the fact that the war was officially over, these were still combat missions against a recognised enemy that was still heavily armed. There were Rules of Engagement in place which basically stated that enemy forces could not be attacked unless they had fired first – terrific.

'Almost to the minute, as we arrived at the jets, the Victor or VC10 would take off in advance and proceed to the refuelling point just north of the Iraq/Turkey border to the extreme eastern edge of Turkey. Also on its way to a similar area would be the USAF E-3A AWACS. This provided complete radar coverage of the entire AOR [Area of Responsibility, affectionately known as "sausage side" to RAF aircrew]. Anything that left the ground or emitted any form of electronic signal could be detected and, if necessary, the E-3A could direct fighter assets to engage and neutralise.

'Back in the Jaguar cockpits, the pilots would load the route into the FIN 1064 navigation system with a "yellow brick". This was a hard drive, roughly the size of a cigarette packet, that contained all the route and target coordinates. Sometimes, the route wouldn't load, so, rather than manually

A Jaguar carries out a low-level photo-run over the rail yards at Mosul. Their surveillance was a regular task for the Jaguars, and such missions enabled Coalition intelligence staff to monitor the reinforcement of Iraqi army units in the north of the country (*Andy Cubin*)

inputting the entire data, the pilot would ask the friendly groundcrew chap to leg it over to another member of the formation and get his "brick".

'Following a successful start-up, normal radio checks were then done and the formation would taxi out. As a personal choice, I would always insist on leading my four-ship formations. This wasn't training, and the younger pilots had more important things to worry about than the complexities of managing formation protocols. At the allocated take-off time, the four-ship would line up in formation on the runway and roll in pairs, with a ten-second stream between pairs. Another advantage of being on the early shift was the air temperature. The cooler morning air meant that the take-off performance of the fully loaded Jaguar was quite reasonable. After lunch, the runway length was frighteningly short.

'We would climb on a northeasterly heading towards Kahramanmaras, colloquially known as "K-town" because no one knew how to pronounce its name properly. "K-town" was the first turning point, and the next heading was east towards Batman, a town northwest of the Iraqi border. Batman also had an airfield with a runway long enough to take a Jaguar. This reassuringly meant that not far over the Iraqi border was a friendly airfield. I don't recall it ever being needed by a Jaguar, but it was nice to have it there.

'We transited at around 20,000 ft towards the tanker. The Jaguar was capable of much higher altitudes, but AAR had to be done using part-throttle reheat – one engine in afterburner – because of the weight of the stores, which meant tanking at a lower altitude than normal.

'AAR was, at best, tricky. The tanker deployed a hose, at the end of which was a basket shaped very much like a shuttlecock. The basket was made of a steel framework joined by pieces of wire, with a canvas ring that had lights built in. Even in smooth air, the basket oscillated somewhat. Once you were stabilised behind the tanker and waiting for the green light to nudge forward and plug in, the secret was to line up the comma of the 20,000 ft [altimeter reading] in the HUD with a mark on the underside of the tanker.

'Once the green light came on, it was a case of smoothly driving forward without looking at the basket. The basket started very close to the right-hand side of the nose, and as the aircraft moved forward, the airflow moved the basket away and upwards from the initial holding position so that, when the probe was about to engage with the basket, everything was in the right place. Once all four jets had been topped up, the tanker remained on station in case of any problems whilst the Jaguars moved off and headed towards the Iraqi border.

'"Weapons hot", was my radio call. We selected the ECM pod on, armed the Phimat dispenser, switched on the AN/ALE-40 flare pack, rotated the recce pod to roll the cameras to their correct fields of view and switched on the guns to "both". Finally, I would lift the cover for the "Clear Aircraft" button – an engine loss with all that load meant a very quick stab of the button to drop everything off the aircraft, leaving enough power from the remaining engine to climb out of Iraq.

'Off to the targets, with two aircraft doing the photography and the other two as top cover. Busy radio from the E-3, the F-16s and the A-10s, as well as the continuous squeaking from the SkyGuardian RWR. The Iraqis were clever, illuminating our aircraft with the acquisition radar of their SA-6 "Gainful" SAMs and forcing us to "duck" to 100 ft or lower to drop under the radar beam. Occasionally the acquisition radar signal would switch to fire control, normally meaning a SAM was in the air. This was usually a ruse. They were trying to get us to fly into the ground.

'It was busy and tense. We usually spent about 40 minutes "sausage side" [over Iraq], and there was certainly nothing that was ever routine about the op. Mission complete, the formation would exit Iraq and transit back to Incirlik, followed by the tanker. On the ground, the camera was downloaded from the pod, processed and the films laid out on the light table to be analysed by the PIs, with the pilots watching and hoping the images were up to the expected high standard – miss the shot at your peril. The combat-ready status of the squadron required the films to be on the table at touchdown +45 minutes – usually easily achieved by a squadron that pulled together and was highly motivated.'

One unforeseen difficulty that emerged was that the camera in the Jaguar reconnaissance pod was optimised for peacetime speeds and heights, and pilots soon found that it did not work so well at operational heights. This had not been an issue during the Gulf conflict, when reconnaissance sorties had been carried out at medium-level.

The problem was that the camera ran the film through the shutter at a speed appropriate to the height and speed of the aircraft – the faster or lower the aircraft flew, the more rapidly the film was driven to generate the required overlap. At normal peacetime speeds and heights – typically 420 knots and 250 ft – this worked well, but when the aircraft was at high speed down at 100 ft or less, the camera mechanism could not drive the film fast enough to match the rate at which the targets passed by. This meant that the image overlap diminished, and if the aircraft descended even lower, it would disappear altogether, leaving gaps between photographs – and the possibility of missing the target altogether.

'The normal RAF recce pod also had a nose camera, obviously pointing forward', continued Sqn Ldr Cubin. 'Every permanent Iraqi military installation had a billboard with an image of Saddam Hussein proudly positioned at the unit's entrance. Natural competitiveness soon generated an extra task of getting the fullest frame nose camera shot of Saddam. This meant flying very low, usually down a road, filming on the nose camera whilst pointing directly towards a military establishment. At these low levels, the overlap couldn't be generated, so it was potluck whether or not a winning image could be guaranteed on a single pass'.

Two photographs showing a low-level flypast of an Iraqi army barracks within the NFZ, and the large image of President Saddam Hussein at the entrance to the facility. The second shot shows the effect of the wing vortices after a high-speed pass by an aircraft flying at such a low height (*Andy Cubin*)

Wg Cdr Tim Hewlett recalled that 'we regularly overflew Mosul, although restricted to a minimum 2000 ft. Once, when we had just landed, one of our PIs wanted me to look at the imagery we had just taken. There were pictures of SA-2 and SA-3 SAMs being unloaded from a Baghdad train in the rail yard. I took the images, taken less than 90 minutes previously, to our US commander. Although pleased, he wanted more pictures immediately. He asked us to "do what you do best" – fly really low and take more images. We launched just ahead of the French and, after refuelling, dropped to low-level and flew over Mosul, this time at just 150 ft. It was such an alien feeling. We flew as fast as possible, but flying so low over a city the size of Norwich was something we never normally did. We got some great images of missiles and their associated radars being unloaded from the train.

'We stayed at Incirlik for about three months before being replaced by another Coltishall squadron. I was very proud of my groundcrew, who had lived in tents beside Incirlik's runway, operated round the clock, worked long hours and did an outstanding job keeping the Jaguars serviceable and the imagery speedily processed.'

Low-level sorties over northern Iraq were not without risk, and aircraft were sometimes targeted by small arms fire. On one mission, flying in a pair, Sqn Ldr Cubin remembered 'we came under small arms fire from a Toyota Land Cruiser. This should not have really come as any surprise, as pretty much everyone in Iraq, even after the main conflict had ended, owned an AK-47. The bullets were clearly visible to me, and there were plenty enough of them in the air as we went through. There were no impacts on either of us though, but by the time I got authorisation to engage the enemy from the AWACS, the bad guys had jumped back into their vehicle and disappeared from sight'.

For the next 18 months, the Jaguar force maintained eight aircraft at Incirlik, with the Coltishall squadrons taking turns to rotate through Turkey for two-month detachments. This arrangement lasted until April 1993, when the Jaguar force took responsibility for operations over the

Balkans. The tasking for Operation *Warden* was then passed to the Harrier GR 7 force, and the first Harrier unit to deploy to Incirlik was No 4 Sqn, which arrived in-theatre in early April 1993 (see *Osprey Combat Aircraft 151 – Harrier GR 7/9 Units in Combat* for details). The first operational Harrier GR 7 mission over Iraq, on 5 April 1993, was accompanied by a Jaguar.

Four years later, in October 1997, having completed their commitment to the Balkans, the Jaguars were deployed again to Incirlik. This time the Coltishall squadrons took turns to provide pilots and groundcrew to support a smaller detachment of four Jaguar GR 3s, which in turn were supported by two VC10K tankers. By now the British participation in *Northern Watch* had been re-named Operation *Resinate North*. The mission profile in the NFZ had changed somewhat since the original Jaguar deployment in 1991, and low-level sorties were no longer permitted over northern Iraq. In order to carry out reconnaissance from medium-level, the EMI reconnaissance pod had been replaced by the Vinten Vicon 18-601 Jaguar Reconnaissance Pod (JRP).

Flt Lt Andy Millikin, a No 6 Sqn pilot who flew Operation *Resinate North* missions between 2000–2002, remembered that 'the Jags were housed in HASs, their small wings carrying two fuel tanks, an AN/ALQ-101-10 jamming pod (known as the "Dash Ten"), a chaff pod

Soviet-made SA-6 'Gainful' SAMs were photographed being unloaded and transferred to Transporter Erector Launcher vehicles in the rail yards at Mosul during an Operation *Warden* mission. The SA-6 was a very effective radar-guided weapon that posed a significant potential threat to Coalition aircraft operating in the NFZ (*Andy Cubin*) and, on top of the wings (as there was no more space), two Sidewinder missiles for self-defence. Finally, there was the Vinten recce pod, which was slung on the centreline under the fuselage. The jet looked great, but the reality was that it was comically overloaded. To add insult to injury, the "Dash Ten" weighed so much that a lead ballast had to be added to the chaff pod on the other wing to balance up the weight, further overloading the poor old girl.

'We were still flying with wet film at this stage in the VINTEN recce pod. This was a large lens "wet" film camera that could be rotated to the left and right of the aircraft by selections in the cockpit. Using simple trigonometry and the aircraft's estimated height above the target, an offset could be planned on JMP (F-16 planning software that was "liberated" by the Jaguar force).

'Therefore, to image a road, for example, a parallel line would be flown to the road, offset by however many feet to ensure the swathe of the camera went through the target. This brought with it two interrelated problems – firstly, any rolling movement by the pilot whilst filming would make the image imperfect or unusable, and secondly, the pilot was required to fly completely straight and level whilst filming. This was never considered good practice over hostile territory, where Iraqi height-finding radars could be heard constantly on our RWRs. Still, it was a necessary evil, and the runs normally only lasted for about 30–40 seconds.'

Jaguar missions were routinely flown as three-ships as part of a larger Combined Air Operation (COMAO). The latter also included four F-15C Eagles as fighter sweep/escort, four F-15E Strike Eagles to engage any Iraqi SAM or AAA systems that attempted to target Coalition aircraft flying within the NFZ and two EA-6B Prowlers to provide EW support and jam any air defence radars. This package was further supported by F-16s or A-10s providing top cover for any CSAR mission mounted by USAF helicopters in the event of an aircraft being lost over northern Iraq. The package, which also included RAF VC10K and USAF KC-135 tankers, was coordinated by an E-3 AWACS. In addition, an RAF Nimrod R1 intelligence gathering aircraft would monitor Iraqi air

A pair of Jaguars GR 3As conduct an Operation *Warden* sortie from Incirlik in April 2002. The nearer aircraft (XJ355) is marked up in No 41 Sqn colours, while the second Jaguar is a No 6 Sqn machine. Both aircraft are carrying Vinten Vicon 18-601 JRPs on their centreline pylons (*US National Archives*)

defence communications, with language experts on board being able to warn Coalition aircraft of Iraqi intentions in real time.

Describing a typical Operation *Resinate North* mission, Flt Lt Andy Millikin recalled that 'there would invariably be a faff with Have Quick, a radio system that "hopped" between frequencies to make it harder to jam. The Jaguar cockpit is well-documented as being an ergonomic nightmare, but the second radio took the biscuit, mounted as it was back to front, such that to the pilot all the selectors and indicators were upside down. It was also blessed with tiny switches and fiddly dials with which to input data.

'I once had to do a total Have Quick reload whilst taxiing for my take-off time. A delayed take-off affected all of the other fighters on the COMAO, and so I was extremely keen not to miss it. I frantically reloaded the radio with 20 different frequencies, cursing an increasing list of people who were either related to, friends of, acquaintances of or anyone who had even passed in the street the person who had designed this infernal radio and installed it back to front. Once that drama was over, going to the NFZ seemed like a piece of cake.

'Normally, the No 2 would quickly take one tonne of fuel onboard to top off, as he was going to wait with the tanker while Nos 1 and 3 did the first recce run. They'd then plug, fill to full and disappear through the "gate" on the Iraqi/Turkish border for 18–25 minutes to do their first recce route, whilst No 2 hung around on the VC10K's wing. Upon their return, No 3 would once again fill up with enough gas to get back and then hightail it off to Incirlik. This was the fast recce run. His imagery would be removed, developed and analysed whilst the COMAO was in the NFZ. If any transgression was found, then a "response option" would be initiated whereby an F-15E destroyed a pre-determined bit of Iraqi military hardware.

'Fast recce was great because we were allowed to ignore the strict speed limits the USAF air traffic controllers imposed and come screaming into the circuit at 600 knots, chuck the jet on the ground, and then speed-taxi to a pre-arranged point, where engineers would disappear under

Three Jaguars, all equipped with Vinten Vicon 18-601 JRPs, close up on a tanker during an Operation *Resinate North* mission in September 2002. The nearest aircraft is painted in the markings of No 54 Sqn. Two of the Jaguars feature the standard grey finish, but the middle aircraft is still camouflaged in earlier ARTF paint (*US National Archives*) the aircraft, remove the film from the recce pod and dash off to have it developed.

'Meanwhile, Nos 1 and 2 would refuel again and then head off on the second recce run. Usually, there were three runs in total. These runs tended to be 18–25 minutes long purely for fuel considerations. We'd use a lot of reheat to get the jets to a fighting speed (useful if you needed to fly defensive manoeuvres) and also height – 25,000 ft was where we'd aim, and once at this magnificent apogee, reheat would be deselected and we'd start a weaving descent down to 21,000 ft rather like a falling leaf. Once there, the burners would go back in and the process repeated, unless the wingman was on a straight and level recce run.

'At this point, the leader became even more intent on the ground, looking for AAA and, more importantly, SAM launches. The Iraqis had modified a lot of their weapons, and the SA-6 could be launched using a CCTV system, with radar illumination only being switched on in the last few seconds. This meant we would be unaware of an attack until it was too late. Spotting such a launch occupied a lot of our time.

'So we'd flutter down and then reheat up around the route. We were working the poor little Jaguar's engines and wings to the edge of their performance, and before long we were heading for the gate and the VC10 for another top-up. Sometimes there would be an attempt at some sort of SAM/AAA engagement. The first time I saw AAA it looked very half-hearted – seven blotches of black about a mile behind us and 1000 ft or so below. In the previous year, my flight commander had had a couple of SA-6s fired at him, but they didn't guide.'

The Jaguar detachment remained at Incirlik patrolling the NFZ for the next five years. During the preparations for the Iraq conflict of 2003, it was envisioned that Jaguars might operate from Turkey into northern Iraq, but the Turkish government refused permission for Coalition aircraft to use its bases during the conflict. As a result, the Jaguars were withdrawn from Incirlik in February 2003, marking the end of 12 years of continuous operational detachments by the Jaguar force.

Photographed over the mountains of eastern Turkey during an Operation *Resinate North* mission in late 2002, Jaguar GR 3A XZ357 of No 41 Sqn is also configured with a Vinten Vicon 18-601 JRP under the fuselage and an AN/ALQ-101-10 EW deception pod on the outer wing pylon. The overwing pylon is fitted, but the launcher rail and AAM are not carried (*US National Archives*)

CHAPTER FIVE

BALKANS – OPERATION
HAMDEN/DENY FLIGHT

16 July 1993–31 July 1995

Soon after the fall of communism in Europe in 1990, ethnic tensions and economic crises triggered the disintegration of the Socialist Federal Republic of Yugoslavia. Nationalist groups within the constituent provinces sought to establish themselves as independent countries and, inevitably, disagreements between ethnic groups led to violence. The next ten years saw a series of brutal civil wars, amongst the most notorious of which was the Bosnian war which erupted in April 1992 when Bosnia-Herzegovina seceded from the Federal Republic. In this new country the ethnic Serb and Croat factions each found themselves outnumbered by Muslims, who made up nearly half the population, and the ethnic tensions were multiplied. As well as military clashes, this conflict was punctuated by large-scale massacres as the Bosnian Serb Army (BSA) carried out a policy of 'ethnic cleansing' of the Muslim population.

NATO had become involved in the Bosnian war in October 1992 when it acted to monitor a NFZ established over Bosnia-Herzegovina by the UN in an attempt to limit the bloodshed. Then, in March 1993,

Jaguar GR 1A XZ113 flies low over the southern Italian countryside during a flight from Gioia Del Colle in late 1984. The lack of missiles on the overwing pylons indicates that this photograph was taken during a training sortie, which was an opportunity for pilots to maintain currency at low-level flying since the Operation *Deny Flight* missions were flown at medium-level. This particular aircraft was later converted to GR 3A standard and is now preserved at the Morayvia museum in Scotland (*Author's Collection*)

NATO Operation *Deny Flight* was initiated after the UN Security Council authorised military action to enforce the NFZ. At this point the RAF despatched six Tornado F 3s (see *Osprey Combat Aircraft 142 – RAF Tornado Units in Combat 1992–2019* for details) with tanker support to join the NATO aircraft patrolling the NFZ.

Despite international attempts at mediation, including the establishment of UN-protected 'Safe Areas' for Bosnian Muslims, the situation in Bosnia deteriorated further, and on 16 July 1993 eight Jaguars from No 6 Sqn, along with 188 ground support staff, were deployed to the Italian air base at Gioia del Colle to provide air support to the UN Protection Force (UNPROFOR) on the ground in Bosnia. A further four aircraft were kept at readiness to deploy from Coltishall if needed.

'Although No 6 Sqn flew the aircraft down to Italy and set up the operation initially, *Deny Flight* was a "Coltishall Wing" commitment', explained Wg Cdr Tim Kerss (OC No 54 Sqn). 'It was comprised of jets from all three squadrons in ground attack fit, apart from two recce birds, one of which was loaded on the centreline weapons station with the BAe F126 "area mapping" photographic reconnaissance pod. The other aircraft had a smaller Vinten Vicon 18-601 JRP. To support the latter aircraft, a detachment from the No 41 Sqn's Reconnaissance Information Centre/Cell also set up an HQ adjacent to the Jaguar line for rapid processing and analysis of wet film photographic reconnaissance.

'Prior to their deployment the aircraft were hastily painted in ARTF light grey, and the only clue as to their owning squadron was the first letter of the white two-letter code displayed on the tail fin and nosewheel door – "E", "F" and "G" were Nos 6, 41 and 54 Sqns, respectively.

'Gioia Del Colle itself was a good airfield from which to operate. At the time of our first deployment, it was used as an F-104 base by the Italian Air Force, although these aircraft were subsequently replaced by Tornados. Initially, the RAF line was just that – a pan on which the Jaguars were lined up, with no protection from the elements, such as searing heat in the summer and heavy rain in the winter. The issue was soon addressed with the placement of temporary canvas shelters, each of which could comfortably house an aircraft, and this, in turn, provided for a significantly enhanced maintenance and ground handling environment.'

Each Jaguar Squadron took responsibility for a two-month period – No 6 Sqn handed over to No 41 Sqn, after which No 54 Sqn took over for November–December 1993, before handing back to No 6 Sqn. This two-monthly rolling sequence continued for the next two years.

'In the first few months we were flying about four pairs of aircraft per day', recalled Wg Cdr Kerss, 'but as and when the requirement intensified, this number could be as high as eight. Flying was limited to daylight hours only, but those days were long, involving early starts (as early as 0400 hrs on some occasions) and late finishes, landing at dusk. In addition, we had two aircraft with pilots on operational "standby", ready to react to any ad hoc tasking that came down from COM5ATAF [Commander, 5th Allied Tactical Air Force], our controlling authority, located at Vicenza, in northern Italy.

'At that time the Gulf War was still fresh in the minds of those on the Jaguar force, so the concept of "medium-level" operations in an aircraft that was most at home "in the weeds" was not new. Indeed, most pilots who had historically participated in Red Flag exercises in Nevada were aware that, from the Americans' point of view, medium-level interdiction would be the future of air warfare, so confident were they that the skies above a battlefield would be secured by superior radar detection, ECM and air defence fighters. Furthermore, at medium- and high-levels, the threat from MANPADS, AAA and small arms is significantly reduced.

A sunshade keeps temperatures bearable as Jaguar GR 1A XZ373 is serviced at Gioia Del Colle in the autumn of 1994. All the underwing stores are easily seen in this view. They are, from left to right, the Phimat chaff pod, two fuel tanks on the inboard pylons and an AN/ALQ-101-10 EW deception pod. A pair of AIM-9Ls are on the overwing pylons (*Author's Collection*)

'A typical day's flying programme comprised sending pairs of aircraft concurrently into the AOR to patrol and work with FACs on the ground, carrying out mock attacks on real targets such as artillery positions as practice for the potential day when "the balloon went up". Although day-to-day sorties involved working with FACs, the UN wanted the option to task aircraft already operating in the AOR to carry out live attacks if suddenly needed.

'Accordingly, the Jaguars were flown in "full war" fit, comprising one or two 1000-lb bombs equipped with freefall tails on the centreline pylon, two overwing AIM-9L missiles, an AN/ALQ-101-10 ECM pod and a Phimat chaff dispenser on the port and starboard outboard wing stations, respectively, and two AN/ALE-40 flare dispensers beneath the fuselage. The aircraft's two 30 mm Aden cannons were each loaded with 120 rounds of HE/AP ammunition. This heavyweight fit, combined with the Jaguar's modest engine power, made for some interesting take-off calculations during the summer months when the high temperatures at Gioia Del Colle meant that even in full reheat the jets were rotating just before the arrestor cables at the far end of the runway!

'A typical sortie over Bosnia would involve a pair of Jaguars working with FACs on the ground. Take-off from Gioia would be as singletons in a 15-second stream to enable the use of full power. A formation take-off would have needed reduced thrust – not ideal with a full weapons load! After departure, we flew a turn onto a northerly heading out over the Adriatic and climbed to about 15,000–20,000 ft. Having signed off with Brindisi Radar, who provided local area traffic information, we made contact with "Magic" – an AWACS-based control unit – for identification and tasking.

'En route, each pilot would get visual confirmation from his wingman that his flare unit was working correctly, after which we would marvel at the beautiful sights of Dubrovnik and the Croatian islands such as Mijet passing below. From this vantage point it was hard to believe that we were looking at a country being ravaged by war.

'More often than not we would enter Bosnian territory over the city of Mostar, and from here the effects of the conflict were more apparent. The collapsed Mostar Old Bridge (Stari Most), which had been blown up, was clearly visible, and as we transited inland, we could see towns and villages that had been utterly "wasted". Entire enclaves of houses stood as empty shells with no roofs, giving the appearance of interlocked squares, and they were nicknamed "Battenbergs" by the pilots. However, apart from occasional fires on the ground, there was little visible evidence from the air of the conflict below.

'Once in the area, we could often clearly see the city of Sarajevo. It was surreal to think that, whilst it appeared peaceful from our vantage point, the truth was exactly the opposite, with horrendous footage from the likes of "Sniper Alley", where innocent civilians literally running the gauntlet were a regular feature on TV screens during news reports seen around the world.'

Flt Lt Shaun Wildey, another Jaguar pilot from No 54 Sqn, later wrote;

'At the time I was at the start of my second tour, aged 25, and designated to attend the next Jaguar QWI course. During my first few missions over Bosnia-Herzegovina in September 1993, I saw the "Battenbergs" and the destruction of this beautiful country. The "Battenberg" was the shape left by the walls of a house when the roof had been burnt off in the orgy of violence when rival factions clashed. Empty and desolate rural villages bore the terrible witness marks of the war.

'We were familiar with the term "ethnic cleansing" from the media. However, the full horror of the phrase was captured during the intelligence briefs, which included reports of how a village had been burnt and the rivers and land poisoned. In one case, I recall that the village elder was hung from a tree and chain-sawed in half. On the television, we'd often see images of refugees pouring from torn lands with a haunted look, and following these briefings I could understand why they wore that mask of numbed grief.'

'Having entered the AOR, continued Wg Cdr Kerss, 'we would head at medium-level to an initial geographical contact point and make R/T [radio] contact with the FAC on the ground. The nationalities of the FACs were many and varied, and depended on geographical location. From memory they were British and French in the vicinity of Sarajevo, Dutch around Srebrenica and Danish in the vicinity of Tuzla. Others included Americans, French and even a contingent of Nigerians.

'Once we had established contact with the FAC and the broad location for the operation, the Jaguars set up a circular pattern, still at

Jaguar GR 1A XZ394/GN over Mostar, in Bosnia-Herzegovina, during an operational sortie in November 1994. Between April 1992 and March 1994, the city had been the scene of heavy fighting between the Croat army and the BSA. This particular Jaguar served for a while as the gate guard for Transair at Shoreham Airport, and it is now preserved at Tattersett, in Norfolk, as part of the RAF Sculthorpe Heritage Centre (*Author's Collection*)

Carrying a single 1000-lb HE bomb, Jaguar GR 1A XZ104 flies over the Adriatic Sea on an Operation *Deny Flight* mission in 1994. The load of a single bomb was the best compromise between arming the aircraft and maximising the time on task by loading the aircraft as lightly as possible. XZ104 still serves as an instructional airframe at Cosford (*Author's Collection*)

about 15,000 ft, with one aircraft on either side of the circle. This pattern became known as "the bicycle wheel", and separating in this fashion enabled the pilots to devote more concentration to the ground whilst still maintaining cross-cover for their wingman. Luckily, the weather on most days was good, with clear skies, but on days when this wasn't the case, we felt very vulnerable knowing that we were flying a predictable pattern and were silhouetted against the cloud above, making visual contact from the ground much easier.

'Once both parties were ready, the FAC would begin talking the pilots' eyes onto the targets, which were invariably Serb artillery or military facilities. To do this they would hone in from large features to small. A typical (abbreviated) "talk-on" would go something like;

'FAC – "Village with river running through and large white church".

'Lead Pilot – "Contact village".

'FAC – "Road leaves village to the east, crossroads 200 metres from village".

'Lead Pilot – "Contact crossroads".

'FAC – "Smaller road from crossroads goes north".

'Lead Pilot – "Contact road".

'FAC – Target is artillery in eastern corner of V-shaped wood 250 metres along road".

'Lead Pilot – "Contact wood. Contact target".

'The pilot would then confirm that his wingman had also sighted the target, before commencing a simulated dive attack with the call "in dry". The word "dry" indicated that although the appropriate weapon-aiming had been called up onto the HUD and the symbology would be placed on, or run through, the target, the aircraft armament switches were safe, so no weapons would be released. The FAC would then respond with the words "Clear Dry", indicating that from their perspective they were happy for the attack manoeuvre to be carried out.

'Some FACs on the ground were equipped with a laser target marker to illuminate the target. This made the life of a Jaguar pilot much easier, as the target would present itself as a symbol in the HUD, having been acquired by the LRMTS seeker head in the aircraft's nose. All that had to be done then was to select the best attack direction and call up the weapon aiming, which would be automatically positioned by the onboard avionics.

'On some occasions, however, the FAC's clearance to attack would be accompanied by warnings like "do not come too low, they are shooting at you". We assumed that this would be small arms fire only, but on one occasion, whilst flying the "bicycle" wheel, an ominous large puff of black smoke suddenly appeared directly between our two aircraft. Given that we were not on offensive ops on that sortie, I decided that it would be prudent for my wingman and I to move out of the area without delay!

'In the "talk-on" example earlier in this chapter, the pilot acquired the target quickly, but at times there were issues making visual contact with a target because what looked to the FAC like a good marker from the ground did not necessarily translate to a good feature from above. Also, estimating distances on the ground could be very subjective. On later missions, however, we also worked with airborne FACs flying in USAF A-10s and US Marine Corps F/A-18s. Generally, this was easier for us because the FAC had the pilot's perspective, and could therefore find good features to lead one's eyes to the target. The counter to this was, of course, that they weren't necessarily aware of the dynamic threat situation on the ground.

'Mission complete, the return to Gioia was simply a reverse of the route into the area. One of the controlling units for the area was operating from a US Navy cruiser sailing in the Adriatic, callsign "Red Crown". Given that day-to-day life for the crew on board ship was pretty mundane, we would often be asked whether we could "pay them a visit"? Fuel permitting, we would oblige. It was always heartening to see the personnel on deck waving enthusiastically as we flew past. However, as any flying supervisor knows, such invitations can be the forerunner to unintended consequences as unplanned events like this can goad young pilots into unsafe territory.

'This was sharply brought into focus when, having flown a "sporty" pass myself, the controller on the radio stated "thanks for the flyby, not bad, but not as low as "Blackcat" section before you – they really took the paint off the decks!" Although my inner mind thought "nice one, boys!", the responsible side felt the need to have a timely word with all my pilots about pushing the limits!'

As well as the close air support (CAS) missions, there was also daily tasking for reconnaissance missions over Bosnia. Unlike the CAS sorties, which were fluid in nature and depended entirely on the requirements of the FAC while the Jaguars were on task, reconnaissance sorties had to be planned meticulously beforehand. The task might specify up to ten targets or areas of interest, and the plan had to cover all of them.

Two aircraft were allocated for the reconnaissance task – one would carry the reconnaissance pod while the other would be in the 'attack' fit and act as an escort. The latter aircraft was necessary because in order to take accurate photographs from medium-level, the Jaguar had to be flown straight and level along the pre-planned track. This involved the pilot being 'heads in' for prolonged periods, which meant he could not keep a good look out for threats such as AAA fire or SAM launches. This responsibility rested with the pilot of the escort aircraft.

Initially, the reconnaissance aircraft was equipped with the bulky EMI Jaguar reconnaissance pod, fitted with the F126 camera (known colloquially as the 'F126 pod'), but this was soon replaced by the new, smaller and technically more advanced LOROP. Because of its greater magnification, the LOROP had the advantage of allowing the aircraft to stand off from the target so that it did not have to actually overfly high threat areas. Being oblique, the LOROP images also had a more three-dimensional quality. However, the stand-off distance brought with it a greater chance of missing the target altogether if the pre-planned track was not flown precisely. A portable GPS unit was fitted to the cockpit's coaming to assist the pilot with accurate navigational information.

By the end of 1993, the Jaguars had flown more than 650 operational sorties over Bosnia. Although no weapons had been expended, the presence of aircraft overhead the UNPROFOR troops had a major impact on the ground situation, as Wg Cdr Kerss explained;

'Invariably, we would stay in the area for as long as possible to act as an airborne show of force, and carry out as many dummy attacks as we could. However, I remember on one occasion flying an early morning mission to overhead Tuzla in northeast Bosnia. The news that morning was that there had been considerable military activity and gunfire overnight. Approaching the area, we made contact with the Danish FAC, who didn't seem too interested in doing the usual FAC target work. I asked him how things were on the ground. "Pretty bad" was the response. "In fact, please stay as long as you can, because as long as you are here the guns go silent". Needless to say, we complied with his request and, instead of wasting fuel with diving manoeuvres, we just continued for as long as we could with a variation of our "bicycle wheel" to maintain mutual support, whilst not becoming a predictable target for ground forces. Once we reached "chicken fuel" – the fuel quantity needed to return to Gioia – we left the area, but the gratitude in the FAC's voice was clear.

'It was at times like these, however, that I and my fellow pilots experienced feelings of intense frustration and impotence. Often, we knew that the situation on the ground was tense and deteriorating, and yet we were sitting in machines armed to the teeth capable of delivering a hammer blow at a moment's notice. But the reality was that that sort of tasking would never come, as such action would have to be approved by the UN all the way from New York, and thereafter by NATO. By the time any such approval came we would be out of fuel and long gone.'

Flt Lt Shaun Wildey echoed the sense of frustration in not being able to intervene;

'I was with another pair on medium-level CAS training with a French Army patrol, "Disney 01", located just outside Sarajevo. When we arrived, they were perched on top of their UN armoured vehicles watching a Serb unit mortar a rival faction's position several hundred metres from them. As we talked to the French guys, while trying to locate the position of the Serbian mortars, the explosions started to move inexorably towards them. We could see the impacts zoning in on the white UN armoured vehicles.

'All of a sudden we received the call, "'Rebel' formation, this is 'Disney 01', standby". We stayed in the area as long as fuel would allow, unable to re-establish contact with "Disney 01". Fearing the worst, we returned to Gioia to file the MisRep [Mission Report]. Some weeks later we found out that "Disney 01" had become the focus for the nationalist Serbs' attention, and they were forced to sit out the brief mortar attack from within their vehicle.'

During 1994, the BSA became increasingly confrontational, attacking some of the UN safe havens and laying an artillery siege to Sarajevo. In response, NATO declared an exclusion zone for heavy weapons around Sarajevo, but this was largely ignored by the BSA. Then, on 16 April, a Sea Harrier FRS 1 – one of a pair flying from HMS *Ark Royal* – was shot down by an SA-7 MANPADS while supporting UNPROFOR troops under attack near Gorazde. This incident emphasised the very real threat to NATO aircraft operating over the Balkans.

The tension continued to rise over the summer, and on 22 September NATO was provoked to respond to BSA aggression by bombing a T-55 tank which was within the Sarajevo exclusion zone. This was very much a political demonstration, rather than a militarily significant strike, and as such it was considered important that it was carried out by non-US aircraft. Two French Mirage 2000s were selected for the task, but they were unable to identify the target. As the day drew on, and with the credibility of NATO coming under question, two USAF A-10s were ordered to strafe the target, while a pair of Jaguars from No 41 Sqn led by Flt Lt Steve Shutt looked on. The dust created by the A-10 cannon strikes enabled him to get 'eyes on' the tank, and he was cleared in to attack it. Shutt scored a direct hit on the T-55 with a 1000-lb bomb, destroying the tank and demonstrating that the operation was indeed a multi-national rather than solely US enterprise.

Despite the marksmanship demonstrated by Shutt near Sarajevo, the BSA continued its offensive action, in particular against the Bihać pocket in northwest Bosnia. Here, the BSA tactics included the use of SSMs. Then, on 19 November, two Serbian J-22 Orao attack aircraft carried out an air strike on Bihać. They were operating from the air base at Udbina, in the Republic of Serbian Krajina, a Serbian-occupied region of Croatia. Since this mission represented a major violation of the NFZ, and therefore a direct challenge to the UN Security Council, the UN requested that NATO carry out a retaliatory strike against Udbina.

Led by the Dutch, the raid on Udbina was a true Coalition effort, involving British, American, Dutch and French assets. The raid itself was planned using reconnaissance imagery provided by the RAF Jaguar detachment. The attack would be opened by strikes by US Marine Corps F/A-18Ds and USAF F-16Cs and F-15Es against SA-6 and AAA defences using AGM-88 High-speed Anti-Radiation Missiles and AGM-65E Maverick missiles, as well as CBU-87s and Mk 82 bombs. Fighter protection would be provided by a pair of Dutch F-16s, and the whole attack package would also be supported by two EF-111A Raven EW jamming aircraft and another pair of AGM-88-armed F/A-18Ds ready to engage any threats that had been missed by the SEAD wave.

Four USAF F-15Es would bomb the runway, while eight aircraft, comprising pairs of French Jaguars, Dutch F-16s, French Mirage 2000s and British Jaguars, would attack the various taxiway intersections. The attack wave would be followed by reconnaissance passes by two British Jaguars, two French Mirage 2000s and two Dutch F-16s.

Although the Jaguar could comfortably carry two 1000-lb bombs, it was reckoned that dropping a stick of ordnance might result in straddling the taxiway, rather than hitting it exactly, so the decision was made to carry

just one bomb on each aircraft. The Tasking Order specifically prohibited the use of an LGB because of the danger of a control malfunction on the weapon which might make it hit the local civilian population – something that had occurred to the RAF Tornado force during the Gulf War. However, this limitation had little effect on the Jaguars, since they did not, at this stage, have an air-designated LGB capability.

Wg Cdr Kerss decided that he ought to lead the British contingent;

'We were very much of the opinion that we had been put onto a "war footing" due to a significant increase in Serbian military activity, and that this would be just the first of numerous missions to quell the rising tide. With this in mind, I felt that it was important to "lead from the front" by flying on this mission, as I didn't expect my pilots to do something that I wouldn't do myself. Accordingly, I liaised with my squadron programmer to ensure that I led this first offensive mission.'

Also in the formation would be Flt Lt Shaun Wildey, who recalled;

'When plans for the mission were drawn up, I was the No 3, and the Boss [Wg Cdr Kerss] and the current QWI, Tom B, were Nos 1 and 2, respectively. It was a great honour to have been selected, although at that stage I was only to have been the airborne spare. As the waiting game played out, while the politicians and military leaders finalised their plans, the QWI had to return to the UK, and I was promoted to the No 2 slot.'

Wildey's place as No 3 was taken by Flt Lt Simon Dowling, and Flt Lt Chris Carder was given the reconnaissance task. Because Carder would largely be 'heads in' during his reconnaissance run, Flt Lt Nev Weir would fly as his escort and keep an eye out for threats in the target area. The attack was due to take place on 20 November, but it was slipped by 24 hours because of a layer of high cloud over the target that would have silhouetted the attacking aircraft, making them more visible from the ground.

'Having taken off as singletons', recalled Wg Cdr Kerss, 'the Jaguars formed up in "battle formation" and headed up the Adriatic to rendezvous with a TriStar tanker of No 216 Sqn, from which we refuelled sequentially from the centreline hose. As Shaun and I took on fuel I could almost feel Simon Dowling in the spare willing one of us to have a problem so that he could take our place! Unfortunately for him it did not happen, and we

Configured in a typical Operation *Deny Flight* fit, Jaguar GR 1A XZ373/GF cruises high over the Adriatic Sea in November 1994. The aircraft crashed seven months after this photograph was taken when USAF exchange pilot Capt Robert Paradis was forced to eject after losing control during an air combat manoeuvring sortie over the Adriatic (*Author's Collection*) left him along with the tanker as we departed for the initial holding point from which we would join the "wagon train" and set course for the target.

'It was after Shaun and I had finished our refuelling that a small, but significant, event demonstrated that people were rooting for us. Normally, our tanking operations were constrained to a race-track pattern within a designated airspace area. However, on this occasion, the TriStar simply flew a straight line up the Adriatic, and as we left a voice on the radio said, "would you like any more fuel and would you like us to follow you or hang around in case you need some on the way home?" In one transmission, the crew had demonstrated that this mission was not going to be constrained by peace-time rules, and that "flexibility" really was the "key to air power." A small gesture, but it felt good!'

Flt Lt Wildey takes up the story;

'Simon stayed with the tanker while the two of us continued with the route, and we pushed to the strike secondary frequency. We had about a 20-minute hold before leaving the gate for the IP, and the attack was underway as we circled to wait for our turn. It was odd to listen to the snippets that were being transmitted back to the waiting bombers. AAA was reported in the target area, but it looked like the [Saab] Giraffe radar had been taken down. This was significant, as this radar was the eyes of the SA-6, and our chances of being engaged had been reduced. I must have cross-checked my switches a hundred times. I vacillated between making the late arm live as we crossed to "sausage-side" or to wait until the normal position of being established in the dive. I can't recall where I did it now, so I expect that training took over.

'We finally committed from the gate and climbed to the mid-twenties [thousand feet]. From a long way out we could see the airfield. The visibility was awesome, and over the target was a large black column of smoke rising well above 10,000 ft. Around it, there were minor palls of

A Jaguar refuels from a No 216 Sqn TriStar K 1 during an Operation *Deny Flight* mission. Sqn Ldr Tim Kerss commented, 'I love this shot. Even though the photograph is marked with canopy reflections, the subject matter is action packed. The Jaguar is venting fuel, there are vortices off the aircraft's wings and the left engine is in part throttle reheat, which we needed to (a) stay in [the basket] and (b) give the necessary throttle response'. Most Operation *Deny Flight* missions were supported by TriStar AAR tankers based at Ancona (*Author's Collection*)

smoke and dust picking out the activity of the ongoing strike. We collapsed the formation into a swept trail and identified our individual DMPIs. Somewhere in this time-slice I think I mismanaged my navigation system. I had no idea of what I had done, or how to rectify the problem, but I found I could not get "Planned" weapon aiming – our primary HUD weapon solution to deliver a bomb. I was concerned that the smoke over the target would prevent a laser lock, thus preventing a decent ranging solution.'

In the lead Jaguar, Wg Cdr Kerss noted as he approached the target that 'the layout of the airfield, sitting low on our left-hand side, looked exactly as we had seen it in the intelligence photographs, with its distinctively shaped angular taxiway clearly visible at the near end. The damage already inflicted was clear to see, with cuts evenly distributed along the length of the main runway, as predicted. The most noticeable features, however, were plumes of dense black smoke from burning tyres and oil fires that had been started on the ground. The smoke was drifting towards our DMPIs on the far taxiway, which was to cause us both an issue during the attack.

'As I prepared to position for the dive attack, I scanned down at the airfield to be greeted by the awe-inspiring sight of the bombs dropped by the preceding Dutch F-16s exploding on the taxiways. This, above all else, brought home that we were involved in a destructive act of war! Approaching my designated tip-in point at 25,000 ft, I double-checked the position of the vital switches – weapon station selected, green bomb-on-station light, video camera on. As my flight path lined up with the taxiway, I over-banked and tipped in, simultaneously calling up "target of opportunity" weapon-aiming in the HUD. Once on the attack heading I "ackled" the target bar onto my DMPI and fired the laser-range finder. A flashing "R" appeared on the left side of the target bar, telling me that the laser was firing, but had yet to lock on.

A still frame from Sqn Ldr Tim Kerss' HUD video of the Udbina attack. The aiming point on the eastern taxiway loop is exactly under the target bar, and the 'R' next to it indicates that the laser ranger is firing (*Author's Collection*)

'I then toggled the final switches to turn the aircraft into an active weapons platform – "stick-top, late arm". I triple-checked the late arm switch – nothing worse than the ignominy of coming home with your bombs still on board due to what is known in the trade as a "switch pigs"!

'Now I had to concentrate on getting the bomb on target. The target bar was holding on the DMPI, with the smaller Computed Impact Point [CIP] marker marching up the HUD towards it. When the two met, providing I was pressing the commit button on the stick-top, the bomb would be released. However, all was not well – due to the drifting smoke, my laser ranger wasn't achieving a lock, and the pesky "R" in the HUD continued to flash. A laser lock gives the weapon-aiming system a direct reading of the all-important slant range to the target – until that is achieved the computer system calculates the slant range using the depression angle of the target bar in the HUD, along with the radio altitude directly below the aircraft. By definition, unless the target elevation is identical to that of the terrain below the Jaguar, the weapon aiming will be erroneous because the computed slant range is incorrect. Hence my prayers at that moment for a lock-on.

'I pressed on in the dive, and just moments before weapon release was rewarded with a solid "R" in the HUD, telling me that the laser range finder had, at last, achieved a lock. My thumb was firmly pressed on the now unguarded stick-top button, and when the CIP marker reached the target bar in the HUD, I heard the familiar and welcome muffled "thud" as the explosive release units released their locks and pushed the bomb away from the centreline pylon. The aircraft juddered and lurched upwards because of the sudden release of its load. Release took place at about 14,000 ft. A brief check of my altitude – 13,500 ft – followed by a hard pull out of the dive ensured that I didn't bust the minimum designated altitude of 12,000 ft. Having safed the switches, I initially climbed straight ahead, before making a sweeping left turn to take up the exit routing.

'As I pulled up, I scanned left to see a scene of utter devastation on the ground – smoke everywhere. I remember three clear thoughts running through my mind virtually simultaneously. The first was "that was just like going to the range at home. So, all that training was realistic after all, and prepared me well for this". The second was "this is surreal". Sitting in the familiar "warm and safe" environment of my Jaguar cockpit, the sight of Udbina airfield ablaze below was like watching an epic film in a theatre. The third was "hope Shaun's okay".'

Wg Cdr Kerss did not have to wait long for an answer. 'The RWR was showing threats', Flt Lt Wildey recalled, 'but I ignored it, hoping that it was the jammers doing their job. Tim tipped in a couple of miles ahead of me, plummeting towards the airfield. I rolled in behind, focusing all my attention and training on achieving the aim. The [bomb]sight steadied on my target and the laser locked. Result! I committed to the attack and then recovered to follow the Boss back upstairs. I jinked as I climbed, looking for AAA. A double explosion on the airfield confirmed that our targets had been hit, and right away a clutch of small AAA puffs materialised a few hundred metres behind us.

'"AAA in our 'six', Boss", I called, and continued to weave away from Udbina. As we left the area, I could see neat craters in the runway. The French had done a great job punching holes in the concrete. All around the airfield, small impact sites could be seen, and the recce jets were flying over, taking the images that confirmed the success of the mission.'

By this time, Wg Cdr Kerss was concentrating on the route home;

'I made a quick jink to get Shaun back into line-abreast battle formation, followed by an orderly transit out of the area via a route to the north of that we had taken in. As we took up our southerly heading back over the Adriatic, we found out that the TriStar crew had been good to their word and were waiting to offer us more fuel if we needed it. We didn't, but it instilled a great feeling of camaraderie amongst the team.

'The return to Gioia was uneventful, and given the circumstances, I led a rather sporty run-and-break into the circuit. To us it seemed fitting, but it did subsequently result in a one-way conversation with the base's operations officer and a promise that we wouldn't do it again. Well, even squadron bosses have to take the flak for their actions from time to time! After landing, as we taxied back to the dispersal, I was amazed at the number of people who lined the taxi route to see us back in. Clearly the likes of CNN had spread the word that this had been a real operational sortie, although judging by the burning tyres that we had witnessed at Udbina, I think that the Serbs had seen the same transmission. There was an air of jubilation as Shaun and I went back into the line hut, and the groundcrew presented us with a couple of hastily-made "bomb dropper" paper medals before insisting that we run the HUD video of the attack for their delectation.

'Of course, the story didn't end there. We all breathed a sigh of relief when Chris Carder and Nev Weir, who were close behind, broke into the circuit. In many respects their mission had been more dangerous than ours, as Chris had had to fly wings-level past the recently bombed airfield in order to get the photographs using the LOROP – potentially a sitting duck for any remaining AAA or MANPADS.

'Once all pilots and aircraft were safely on the ground, the five of us gathered for a post-mission photograph before departing to our accommodation at the Hotel Svevo in Gioia town for an evening of celebration. Although everyone was telling me to let my hair down, I'm sure that I wouldn't be the first to admit to feeling a deep sense of anticlimax, and the need to reflect a while after a first dip into the world of real offensive operations.'

Rather than being the starting point for further attacks by NATO aircraft, the strike against Udbina turned out to be a one-off event. However, Wg Cdr Kerss judged it to be a landmark for two reasons;

'Firstly, it was the largest joint mission of NATO aircraft since the alliance's formation, and it was heralded as a great success by the UN and the commander of 5th ATAF. However, secondly, the raid did highlight the limitations and potential inaccuracies of using "dumb bombs" to hit a point target. Had it not been for the rules imposed for the mission, the use of laser-guided munitions would have been a far better option.'

In fact, the introduction of a precision strike capability for the Jaguar was under development, and it would shortly be deployed into the Balkan theatre. With the coming of advanced technology systems, such as the Jaguar–TIALD combination that enabled the use of highly effective guided munitions, Wg Cdr Kerss believed that 'the face of modern air warfare had changed forever'.

The five pilots who participated in the Udbina airfield strike on 21 November 1994 enjoy a beer at Gioia Del Colle after the mission. They are, from left to right Flt Lts Simon Dowling (No 3/airborne spare) and Shaun Wildey (No 2), Sqn Ldr Tim Kerss (Leader) and Flt Lts Chris Carder (reconnaissance) and Nev Weir (reconnaissance escort) (*Author's Collection*)

CHAPTER SIX

BALKANS – OPERATION *VULCAN/DELIBERATE GUARD*

29 August 1995 – 2 July 1998

Jaguar GR 1A XX974 taxies out at Gioia Del Colle for a sortie over Bosnia-Herzegovina in 1994–95. Unusually, it is loaded with two 1000-lb HE bombs under the fuselage – a single bomb was a more typical load. Later modified into a GR 3A, this aircraft is preserved in the Piet Smits collection at Baarlo in the Netherlands
(Crown Copyright/MoD)

Back in Britain, the need for a better precision bombing capability for the Jaguar had been recognised in early 1994, leading to the issue in June that year of UOR 41/94 to upgrade 12 aircraft to enable them to carry the GEC-Marconi TIALD and Paveway II LGB. The UOR also specified that the TIALD/LGB capability should be provided within 12 months. The project was driven by Sqn Ldr Pete Birch, OC Standards and Evaluation at Coltishall, working closely with the Defence Evaluation and Research Agency (DERA) and RAF engineers at St Athan, in Wales.

The modifications to the aircraft included provision of the Military Standard 1553 digital databus, as well as a Marconi 1:1 HUD, a colour multi-function display and a new stick top. Largely thanks to the efforts of Sqn Ldr Birch, a number of aircraft were modified to this new Jaguar GR 1B standard in short time. The first example was converted at Boscombe Down, in Wiltshire, by DERA engineers, the second at Boscombe Down by a mix of DERA and RAF engineers and the remaining aircraft at St Athan by RAF engineers. Seven modified aircraft had been delivered by mid-November. Four QWIs were involved in the trials work at Boscombe Down in the autumn of 1994 and an operational capability was achieved in early 1995.

Three Jaguar GR 1Bs deployed to Gioia Del Colle in March 1995. Although the aircraft could carry both a TIALD pod and an LGB for a self-designated attack, sorties were also flown to practise cooperative designation – in other words, the Jaguars worked in pairs, with one aircraft designating the target while the other dropped the bombs.

Meanwhile, the situation in Bosnia-Herzegovina deteriorated during the spring of 1995, and as the fighting intensified Sarajevo was shelled again by the BSA. After initial reluctance on the part of the UN, it was agreed that some sort of military intervention was needed. On 25 and 26 May USAF F-16s and Spanish EAF-18As targeted the BSA ammunition depot at Pale with LGBs. Then, during July, the BSA seized the UN declared Safe Areas around Gorazde, Zepa and Srebrenica, taking UNPROFOR personnel hostage. With tensions mounting in the Balkans, No 6 Sqn prepared to hand over responsibility for the offensive support role within Operation *Deny Flight* to Harrier GR 7s of No 4 Sqn.

Aircraft from No 4 Sqn began to arrive at Gioia del Colle in late July, and the unit's first mission, with a Jaguar leading a pair of Harriers, was flown on 25 July. By 1 August 1995, 12 Harrier GR 7s had relieved the Jaguars of No 6 Sqn. However, at that stage, the TIALD pods had not yet been cleared for use on the Harrier, leaving No 4 Sqn without an organic precision attack capability. Instead, the two TIALD-equipped Jaguar GR 1Bs were held on standby at Coltishall, ready to deploy to Gioia del Colle to act as target designators in the event that the Harriers were called upon to carry out LGB attacks.

One Jaguar remained in-theatre at Gioia Del Colle until mid-August, and a composite Jaguar/Harrier formation was able to practise the tactics for cooperative laser attacks on 14 August before the aircraft returned to Coltishall. The Jaguar/Harrier concept had already been trialled and proven, including a live bomb drop earlier in the year when Sqn Ldr Birch laser-designated a target for Harrier pilot Flt Lt Al Pinner at the Luce Bay air weapons range in Scotland. In addition to designating for LGB attacks, the TIALD aircraft could also be used to mark targets for the Harriers to attack with freefall weapons – in this case the laser mark gave the Harrier's weapon aiming system an accurate update, which enabled a more precise bomb delivery.

OPERATION *VULCAN*

NATO artillery bombarded BSA positions near Sarajevo on 28 August, and offensive action by NATO aircraft against the command-and-control structures started two days later. The Jaguar GR 1B pilots at Coltishall waited for the order to deploy as the Harrier detachment at Gioia del Colle readied itself for action.

'The call to deploy came late on the afternoon of 29 August', wrote Sqn Ldr Alex Muskett of No 6 Sqn. 'Only one aircraft was ready, so I departed Coltishall at around 1700 hrs and, having refuelled in Nice, arrived at Gioia del Colle that evening at around 2100 hrs. "Blakey" [Flt Lt Simon Blake] was to follow me the following morning, and on his arrival, was thrown straight into planning for an operational sortie that same afternoon'.

Flt Lt Simon Blake later recalled that 'I ended up being the first non-QWI to gain TIALD Combat Ready status. I was the No 6 Sqn Qualified Flying Instructor/Instrument Rating Examiner, and "Musky" [Sqn Ldr Muskett] was one of the flight commanders. Having flown the last of the Jaguars to leave Gioia on 31 July 1995 on hand over to the Harrier force, I had been on leave for most of August (although we had a standby roster to send a couple of "spikers" back if required).

'On returning to work, I spent 24–25 August regaining TIALD currency, which proved insightful. After the Sarajevo bombing, it became clear that NATO was going to react. On 29 August, I was tasked to take a jet and pod to Boscombe Down for harmonisation, as we did not have the facility at Coltishall – "Musky" flew the other jet directly to Italy. That took most of the day, and I ended up flying back very late that same evening with a temporary canopy seal repair (a Bic biro!) that ended up lasting the next few weeks. I had enough time to get home, pack a bag and then get up early on 30 August to meet a VC10K out of Brize Norton, which tanked me to the French FIR [flight information region] boundary, at which point I reckoned I had enough fuel to get direct to Gioia. I landed straight into the [operational] plan[ning].'

The British participation in the air strikes, codenamed Operation *Vulcan*, started on 30 August with two waves of attacks against the ammunition storage facility at Hadzici and the BSA headquarters at Pale. Both of these targets were large arrays consisting of around 20 individual bunkers or buildings, each of which constituted a separate target with a specific aiming point. In the case of Hadzici, there were also two other target sites in close proximity – a military vehicle repair facility and a military equipment storage site. Target acquisition would therefore be complicated.

The RAF aircraft formed part of five large strike packages mounted throughout the day, designated Alpha to Echo, which included SEAD assets and fighter escort for the strike aircraft. The first RAF formation to launch, as part of Strike Package Charlie, was a six-ship comprising two Jaguars each leading two Harriers against Hadzici. Sqn Ldr Muskett led the first section while Flt Lt Blake was the target designator for the second pair of Harriers. The Jaguars were equipped with TIALD pods and each Harrier was armed with two Paveway II 1000-lb LGBs.

'Our Standard Operating Procedure was for the Jaguar to effectively lead with the GR 7 guys acting as lookouts, using their ARBS [Angle Rate Bombing System] as a situational awareness tool', recalled Flt Lt Blake. 'This proved very effective, and allowed us to stay "heads in" [the cockpit] a lot. This was necessary as the Jaguar had no auto pilot or height/heading hold. Thus, we acquired the target and then lased, with the GR 7 guys confirming a good "spot", and also helping with finessing the track (which on occasion proved very helpful)'.

Harrier pilot Sqn Ldr Andrew Suddards commented further that 'if the Jags were firing their lasers, we could put our TV in scan mode and, with the same [laser] codes entered, we could confirm that the Jags were lasing the correct target. We used verbal confirmation codewords too, such as "Six seconds, three seconds to bomb release", with the Jags confirming "Happy" or "No joy". Our weapon-aiming system had auto release on TV or laser lock, which gave us the timing countdown. This meant we were pretty well placed to have double confirmation – verbal from the Jags, and what we were seeing on our screens – that the right target was being lased'.

Over Bosnia, the combined formation encountered intermittent layers of low cloud, and on reaching the vicinity of Hadzici, Muskett could see that the target itself was obscured by banks of broken cloud. 'I was unable to identify my target on the first pass', he admitted, 'so I was forced into a re-attack, allowing "Blakey" and his pair to sneak in ahead, and so become the first single-seat RAF pilot to prosecute an attack using an airborne laser-designator on operations.'

Following just two minutes behind the first section, Blake found that the cloud had moved sufficiently to allow him a clear view of the target, thus giving his Harrier pilots the opportunity to drop their weapons successfully. Muskett, too, was able to acquire the target on his second pass, and the first pair were also able to deliver their bombs accurately. It was with some irony that the three Qualified Flying Instructors dropped the first bombs of the campaign, rather than the three QWIs in the first section.

The attack had been a complete success, and as Sqn Ldr Suddards pointed out, 'being one of the first sorties and first buddy lasing efforts, we were delighted that things seemed to work well. The Jag was able to operate in a cleaner, lighter fit, and therefore had good medium-level performance. The Harrier had better inherent medium-level performance, and it easily coped with the extra weight and drag of the bombs'.

The second RAF wave on 30 August was part of Strike Package Delta (the fourth of the large multi-national air strikes), for which No 4 Sqn Harrier pilot Sqn Ldr Stuart Atha was the overall package commander. Sqn Ldr Muskett, flying his second sortie of the day in the Jaguar, led a pair of Harriers flown by Atha and US Marine Corps exchange pilot Maj Mike Hile. Both No 4 Sqn aircraft were armed with freefall bombs.

'On my second mission that day', recalled Muskett, 'I was supporting two Harriers attacking Pale, the headquarters of the BSA. The lead Harrier was flown by Sqn Ldr Stu Atha. Unbeknownst to us, less than ten minutes before we attacked, a French Air Force Mirage [2000D] targeting the same facility had been shot down. Pale's defences were, therefore, ready and waiting, and we were fired on by two SA-7 [MANPADS], which were fortunately spotted by Stu's wingman, Mike Hile'. The Harriers were loaded with freefall bombs, and the plan was for Muskett to mark the target with the TIALD pod so that the Harriers could update their weapon-aiming system using an accurate laser mark.

Sqn Ldr Atha described how 'after a challenging descent through cloud, we transited across Bosnia, passed Sarajevo and joined the tail of Strike Package Delta. As we approached the target area near the Serbian stronghold of Pale, the scene was reminiscent of World War 2 footage.

TIALD-equipped Jaguar GR 1B XX748 leads an LGB-armed Harrier GR 7 over the Adriatic Sea during an Operation *Vulcan* sortie in September 1995. Both aircraft are also armed with AIM-9L Sidewinder AAMs for self-protection. Typically, one Jaguar would work with a pair of Harriers, designating targets for each aircraft in turn. From the outset, Operation *Vulcan* was a joint effort by the Jaguar GR 1Bs of No 6 Sqn and the Harrier GR 7s of No 4 Sqn. The Jaguars used the TIALD pod to laser designate targets for the Harriers to bomb. Good rapport between the Jaguar and Harrier pilots meant that the mixed formations were very effective (*Andrew Suddards*)

Plumes of smoke billowed into the air and many of the ammunition storage buildings and factories surrounding the town were already ablaze, with flames leaping high into the sky.

'"Musky" fired his laser at the designated target, helping me lock the Harrier GR 7's Dual Mode Tracking system onto the ammunition storage shed. With seconds to go, my thumb was hovering above the control column, ready to press the bright red circular bomb release button, when Hile spotted the launch of two missiles from a spot high up on the side of Mount Igman, north and west of the target area. Responding to Hile's warning call, I aggressively manoeuvred my aircraft and dispensed flares – the ingrained response drilled into all Harrier pilots.

'As I threw my aircraft around the sky, I looked over my shoulder to see, disappointingly, the upwards expanding smoke trail of two SAMs continuing to arc towards me. Readying myself for the well-practised Harrier endgame manoeuvre, which involves the pilot conducting a violent barrel roll around the missile to generate sufficient miss distance to survive, both missiles, rather disconcertingly, disappeared. The end of the smoke trail marked the end of the rocket-assisted boost phase of the launch, but not the end of the missile's flight. This had not been mentioned in the tactic's manual – how do you fight a missile you cannot see? After a tense couple of seconds the missiles reappeared thankfully as they automatically detonated some 2000 ft from the aircraft.'

Having evaded the missiles, the Harrier pilots regrouped and manoeuvred to re-attack the target from a different direction. Meanwhile, Muskett had continued south of the target and was too far away to rejoin the Harriers. The re-attack had mixed success, with Hile successfully destroying his target but Atha experiencing a weapons system failure that meant he could not release his bombs.

31 August brought more of the poor weather that would hamper much of the campaign, with layered cloud across most of Serbia and Kosovo and fog covering much of the terrain. The events of the day also highlighted the delicate reliability of the early TIALD pods, which would also cause problems. The two TIALD Jaguars launched from Gioia del Colle, each leading a pair of Harriers to bomb an ammunition storage area at Ustikolina. Unfortunately, Sqn Ldr Muskett suffered a TIALD pod failure

The TIALD pod is clearly visible beneath the fuselage of the Jaguar GR 1B in this photograph of a Jaguar/Harrier pair over the Adriatic Sea in September 1995. Although the weather in-theatre made laser-designated attacks difficult to achieve, it was reckoned the combined Jaguar/Harrier attacks in the Balkans achieved a success rate of more than 80 per cent (*Mark Linney*)

soon after take-off and returned to base, leaving Flt Lt Blake to cover the targets for both pairs of Harriers. However, the mission had to be aborted when it became clear that the weather over Bosnia was unsuitable, forcing all aircraft to return with their weapons on board.

That evening, Gen Bernard Janvier, the commander of UN forces in Bosnia, ordered the bombing to cease initially for 24 hours (and later extended to four days) while negotiations were held with the Bosnian Serb leader Gen Ratko Mladic. However, when these negotiations came to nothing, offensive action was resumed at 1305 hrs on 5 September. That afternoon, Muskett led three Harriers against the ammunition depot at Ustikolina, once again in marginal weather.

As they approached the target area, the aircraft came under fire from AAA, but it was actually the low clouds that prevented Muskett from finding the target with the TIALD pod, causing the mission to be aborted. Blake was luckier with the weather conditions 30 miles further to the east and was able to designate ammunition storage bunkers at Visegrad for two Harriers that scored direct hits. 'One hit was spectacular, and the building had clearly contained some other ordnance', commented Blake. A second attempt against Ustikolina the following day, this time involving AAR support, was once again thwarted by the weather over the target area. So, too, was a follow-up operation against Visegrad.

The first target on 7 September was the radio relay station at Doboj, with two Jaguar–Harrier pairs tasked for the mission. This time it was Flt Lt Blake who suffered a TIALD pod failure, leaving Sqn Ldr Muskett to 'spike' for both Harriers. Difficulty in acquiring the correct aiming point in an area that had already been heavily attacked meant that the bombs all missed the target.

On his second sortie of the day, Muskett marked Visegrad ammunition storage bunkers for two Harriers. Each aircraft dropped two LGBs, and this time both pilots scored direct hits on their targets. After supporting this successful attack, Muskett refuelled from a TriStar tanker before

The officers and aircrew of No 4 Sqn and No 6 Sqn who took part in Operation *Vulcan*, photographed after hostilities had ceased. Flt Lt Simon Blake is standing second from the left and Sqn Ldr Alex Muskett is seated sixth from the left. Standing second from the right is Flt Lt Geraint Herbert from No 41 Sqn, who was the back-up TIALD pilot. The aircraft, in appropriate stores configurations, make an impressive backdrop (*Mark Linney*)

Groundcrew prepare Jaguar GR 1A XZ364 for its next reconnaissance mission over Bosnia-Herzegovina as part of Operation *Vulcan*. The aircraft is carrying an EMI Jaguar reconnaissance pod on its centreline, plus a Phimat chaff pod, two fuel tanks on the inboard pylons and an AN/ALQ-101-10 EW deception pod. Finally, it has a pair of AIM-9Ls on the overwing pylons (*Crown Copyright/MoD*)

returning to the operational area to rendezvous with four more Harriers for an attack on an EW deployment site at Tuzla. The target was an array of radars sited within berms that were defended by several AAA emplacements. LGBs dropped by the first pair caused severe damage, and the site was destroyed by the second pair. Muskett returned to Gioia del Colle after a long day and a 3 hr 40 min flight.

On 8 September, Flt Lt Blake in the TIALD Jaguar led three Harriers against Jahorina, some 12 miles southeast of Sarajevo, but once again the mission was abandoned because of a combination of clouds partially obscuring the target and, ultimately, a TIALD pod failure.

A radio relay station at Tuzla was proving to be an elusive target, despite the attention of both the Harriers and French Mirage 2000Ds. According to Sqn Ldr Atha, 'a friendly rivalry had grown between the French and British squadrons. This was best exemplified by a "race" to be first to destroy an important and particularly large communications mast north of Tuzla – a mission that became known as "Operation Timber". Both nations had made a number of attempts that had been thwarted by the weather.'

Two attempts by the Harriers to bomb the mast on 9 September were abandoned because the target was obscured by clouds, and the first mission the following day was scrubbed when Blake experienced fumes in the cockpit of his Jaguar. Later, on 10 September, Sqn Ldr Muskett set out, leading a pair of Harriers for a second attempt against the mast. When they arrived in the target area, the formation was re-tasked to a CAS target, but this second target proved too difficult to locate with the TIALD pod so the aircraft were sent to a TriStar tanker to refuel.

'I have a vague recollection of jousting away like an idiot in front of my two GR 7 mates and a whole bunch of Sea Harriers', recalled Muskett. 'The best bit was that the Sea Harriers slowly reached "Bingo" one by one and had to peel off back to the ship – it was very much a case of "Out the way, RAF officers coming through" which we found highly amusing!'

The three aircraft then returned to Tuzla and their original target. Here, they were joined by three more Harriers, each carrying two 1000-lb freefall bombs. With dusk fast approaching, the five Harriers carried out an almost simultaneous attack on the site. 'Unsurprisingly', recorded Sqn Ldr Atha, 'the mast was successfully downed, and as the squadron aircraft also carried reconnaissance pods, a photograph of it lying on the ground was taken and subsequently sent to the French detachment, allowing us to declare "Operation Timber" complete'. The Jaguar and the five Harriers landed in the dark to signal the end of sorties that had lasted more than three-and-a-half hours.

The next morning (11 September) it was the turn of Flt Lt Blake to lead the first mission of the day in the TIALD Jaguar, but the sortie had to be abandoned because there was no SEAD support available. On his second mission, Blake was the designator for four Harrier GR 7s, each of which was armed with two LGBs, targeting Hadzici ammunition depot. Four different buildings within the depot complex had been selected as targets for the four Harriers.

For his third mission of the day, Blake was joined by Muskett to lead four Harriers against the ammunition depot at Ustikolina. During this attack, Muskett carried out two 'spiking' runs on targets for one of the Harriers, which dropped a single LGB on each pass. Meanwhile, Blake marked the targets for a pair of Harriers led by Maj Hile, although he experienced some problems with his TIALD pod. As he explained, the laser 'spot kept moving. Maj Hile talked me back on as the bomb was already falling, and the Paveway II had just about enough energy to knock on the door before hitting it!' Blake recorded another direct hit, albeit a lucky one.

The Hadzici ammunition depot, which was by now becoming a familiar target, was struck again on 12 September. During the attack on a hardened bunker, Muskett lost tracking with his TIALD pod, which then failed, and both bombs in the air fell short. In the second Jaguar, Blake was marking a storage bunker. 'This target was weaponeered with experts from MoD', explained Blake. 'The result was the correct fusing to penetrate the bunker and just blow the doors out, leaving a puff of smoke from the rear ventilation shaft. Very satisfying!' He continued, 'the whole detachment was a great success, and became known as the "Italian Job" – with some obvious references from the film acting as part of a soundtrack to a very cheesy video that was put together, including the "blowing the doors off" from this sortie'.

The attack on Hadzici was the last successful 'live' mission of Operation *Vulcan*. The following day, 13 September, a follow-up attack on the Ustikolina ammunition depot by two Jaguars and four Harriers was aborted because of the weather conditions. A ceasefire came into effect on 14 September. During the two weeks of the operation, the Jaguars had flown 28 operational sorties and designated for 48 LGBs dropped on 19 targets. 'I recall that we calculated at the time that in excess of 80 per cent of attacks were successful, with the odd failure primarily due to faults with the TIALD pod', noted Sqn Ldr Muskett.

With the end of the bombing campaign, air operations over Bosnia returned to the routine of reconnaissance and CAS for UNPROFOR. Jaguars were not required for either mission. 'After this it became very tedious as there was an effective ceasefire and a lot of diplomacy', commented Flt Lt Blake. 'We recovered back to Coltishall via Istres on 25 September. In the interim, [Flt Lt] Geraint Herbert had been sent out to help us, but he never got to fly'.

OPERATION *DELIBERATE GUARD*

The Harrier force continued supporting the NATO peacekeeping Implementation Force, and its successor, Stabilisation Force (SFOR), in Bosnia for another two years. During that time No 41 Sqn deployed two Jaguars, flown by Wg Cdr Chris Harper (OC No 41 Sqn) and Flt Lt

Geraint Herbert, for the period 23–27 September 1996 to practise mutual designation procedures under operational conditions.

The Jaguar force returned to the Balkans more permanently on 3 February 1997, when the Harriers of No 3 Sqn handed back responsibility for Operation *Deliberate Guard* to the Jaguars of No 41 Sqn, now under the command of Wg Cdr John Moloney. Although six Jaguar GR 1As had deployed to Gioia Del Colle on the 3rd, there was a week's delay in taking over the reconnaissance commitment from the Harriers when No 41 Sqn encountered problems with the Vinten Vicon 18-601 JRP.

At this stage TIALD-capable aircraft were not deployed to Gioia Del Colle, but a further six Jaguars were held in readiness at Coltishall in case reinforcements were needed. A TriStar tanker based at Ancona was still available to support the Operation *Deliberate Guard* detachment, and further flexibility was achieved with the receipt of clearance for the Jaguars to use French KC-135FR tankers that were also operating in-theatre as part of the NATO force.

The Jaguar detachment was taken over by No 54 Sqn (commanded by Wg Cdr Russ Torbett) on 24 March 1997. Unfortunately, new rules introduced after an F/A-18 Hornet had inadvertently dropped a Mk 82 bomb over Bosnia prohibited 'dry' attacks against targets in which the whole attack profile, except actual weapon release, was practised. Previously, Jaguar pilots had carried out numerous dry attacks against targets under the control of FACs, which ensured that they were well practised in the delivery profile from medium-level and were ready to use their expertise should it be needed. Now they would not be quite so ready.

No 6 Sqn, commanded by Wg Cdr Mick Roche, held responsibility for Operation *Deliberate Guard* from 30 May to 23 July 1997, flying 122 CAS and 124 reconnaissance sorties in that time. By then, all six aircraft within the detachment had been modified to Jaguar GR 1B standard. The first Jaguar GR 3s fitted with TIALD pods deployed during the No 41 Sqn detachment in the next roulement, giving the Jaguar detachment a greatly improved operational capability. There was no longer any need to practise 'dry' dive attacks from medium-level, since pilots could now concentrate on perfecting new TIALD/LGB tactics. Cooperative designation attacks were also practised by No 6 Sqn when the Harrier GR 7s of No 1 Sqn briefly operated in-theatre, embarked in HMS *Invincible*, between 8–10 December 1997.

Jaguar GR 1A XZ364 (which saw extensive combat in Operation *Granby*) taxies out at Gioia Del Colle at the start of a reconnaissance mission over Bosnia-Herzegovina, while in the background other aircraft are readied for their next sortie. The Jaguar force took responsibility for supporting SFOR in Bosnia-Herzegovina from February 1997 until July 1998 (*Crown Copyright/MoD*)

Mission tasking for Operation *Deliberate Guard* was typically for eight sorties a day, although in surge periods – during the Bosnian local elections in early October 1997, for example – this was increased to 12 (in three waves of four aircraft). The tasking was 40 per cent CAS, 40 per cent reconnaissance and 20 per cent ready force practice. Using the TIALD pod, the Jaguars might also be called upon for 'Hotspot' tasks – real-time back up to a ground incident using TIALD to monitor and record events, and to use LGBs if necessary. An additional task was the Entities Compliance Check mission, another monitoring function that could be carried out using the TIALD's video camera.

The Jaguar squadrons continued to take responsibility for Operation *Deliberate Guard* in the sequence No 6 Sqn, then No 41 Sqn and then No 54 Sqn. The British commitment reduced from 6 April 1998 to just four aircraft, in parallel with a US drawdown of SFOR. However, although the size of the NATO force in the Balkans was being made smaller, NATO countries agreed to mount Exercise Determined Falcon on 15 June 1998. Its aim was to demonstrate the resolve of NATO, and its ability to deploy air forces quickly into the theatre.

In all, 82 aircraft participated, representing all the countries in NATO except Luxembourg and Iceland (which do not have their own air forces) and Canada, which was unable to detach aircraft to Europe at such short notice. The huge formation of aircraft, which included four RAF Jaguars, refuelled over the Adriatic Sea, before flying over Albania and the former Yugoslav Republic of Macedonia. Despite this impressive show of force, the NATO news bulletin noted that 'in Padesh, Albania, residents and Kosovan refugees who watched the NATO exercise today said it probably was not enough to stop the bloodshed in Kosovo'.

Operation *Deliberate Guard* became Operation *Deliberate Forge* on 20 June 1998, and on 3 July four Harrier GR 7s deployed to Goia del Colle to replace the Jaguars there.

A pair of Jaguar GR 3As patrol above cloudy skies during Operation *Deliberate Guard* in support of the SFOR in Bosnia-Herzegovina during 1997–98. Although the situation in the country had largely stabilised by that time, ethnic tension in Kosovo was building steadily. Once again, however, the Jaguar would be replaced in-theatre by the Harrier just before hostilities broke out (*Crown Copyright/MoD*)

APPENDICES

COLOUR PLATES COMMENTARY

1

Jaguar GR 1A XX764/J of No 14 Sqn, Brüggen, West Germany, 1976

The Jaguar was remarkable for being the RAF's first and last single-seat nuclear strike aircraft. XX764 of No 14 Sqn is loaded with a British WE177 nuclear weapon, as it would have been armed for Quick Reaction Alert (QRA). Five WE177-equipped aircraft were held at 15 minutes readiness 24 hours a day, 365 days a year throughout the decade of Cold War Jaguar operations at Brüggen. This aircraft is painted in the early camouflage scheme, with light grey undersides, before wraparound camouflage was introduced later that year. Happily, nuclear QRA Jaguars were never launched in anger, so the aircraft actually never flew in this configuration. XX764 is preserved at Enstone airfield in Oxfordshire.

2

Jaguar GR 1A XX962/X (Operation *Granby*), JagDet Muharraq, Bahrain, January 1991

The first few missions during Operation *Granby* were flown in the standard Cold War configuration, with two underwing fuel tanks and two bombs carried on the fuselage centreline pylon. XX962's Arabian woman nose art was one of the first to be painted onto a Jaguar by Cpl Paul Robins, who later wrote 'after a lengthy search of the back streets of Bahrain, I located a supply of suitable waterproof acrylics. The Arabian woman artwork, with two left feet, which followed shortly thereafter was a trial of my new-found assets'. The five bomb silhouettes indicate the number of operational sorties that had been carried out by the aircraft at that early stage in the war.

3

Jaguar GR 1A XZ367/P (Operation *Granby*), JagDet Muharraq, Bahrain, January 1991

When fitted with a centreline tank and tandem beams on the inner stores pylons under each wing, the Jaguar could be armed with four 1000-lb HE bombs. XZ367, however, is carrying just two CBU-87s (largely obscured by the AN/ALQ-101-10 deception pod), for the weapon was too long to fit more than one onto a tandem pylon. The Jaguar was unusual in mounting the Sidewinder launchers on overwing pylons, and during Operation *Granby* the aircraft carried AIM-9L AAMs for self-defence. Its *DEBBIE* artwork was again by Cpl Paul Robins, who described how as he 'grew in confidence, and with a limited amount of free time, *DEBBIE* took shape – she was named after the wife of a member of the Jaguar engineering team'. The mission symbols record the number of bombs dropped from the aircraft by late January 1991 – 26 1000-lb HE bombs and two CBU-87s.

4

Jaguar GR 1A XZ119/Z (Operation *Granby*), JagDet Muharraq, January 1991

After the early missions during Operation *Granby*, the Jaguar stores configuration for offensive support missions was standardised as depicted here, with a centreline fuel tank, weapons carried on the inboard underwing pylons, AIM-9L on the overwing pylons, an AN/ALQ-101-10 deception pod mounted on the left outer wing pylon and a Phimat chaff pod on the right outer wing pylon. As well as the *Katrina Jane* artwork, XZ119 carries the names of the three most junior pilots in the Jaguar Detachment beneath its windscreen. This aircraft has been preserved and repainted in its Operation *Granby* colours (with 13 1000-lb HE bomb symbols, 25 CBU-87 symbols and one CRV7 symbol) and put on display in the Military Aviation Hangar at the National Museum of Flight in East Lothian, Scotland.

5

Jaguar GR 1A XZ118/Y (Operation *Granby*), JagDet Muharraq, Bahrain, January 1991

Clearance to use the CRV7 rocket was granted in late January 1991, although the weapon-aiming software was not delivered until much later in the conflict. As a result, early firings of the rocket were not particularly accurate, and it was withdrawn until the correct software arrived. The rockets were carried in 19-round pods loaded onto the inboard underwing pylons, which are obscured in this view by the AN/ALQ-101-10 pod. The nose art by Cpl Paul Robins depicts a character from the satirical comic *Viz*. The eventual tally of mission markings for this aircraft recorded 12 1000-lb HE bomb, 18 CBU-87 and two CRV7 sorties – as well as an AIM-9L that was fired accidentally!

6

Jaguar GR 1A XZ367/P (Operation *Granby*), JagDet Muharraq, Bahrain, February 1991

This Jaguar was initially painted with *DEBBIE* artwork (see Profile 3), but as Cpl Paul Robins later recalled, 'unfortunately this creation was not to last, and subsequently, due to a breakdown in communications, Chris [Froome] was asked to replace it with the white rose'. It is depicted here in the standard JagDet load of a centreline fuel tank, four 1000-lb HE bombs on tandem beams, overwing AIM-9Ls and AN/ALQ-101-10 and Phimat pods. During Operation *Granby* this aircraft completed 18 1000-lb HE bomb and 22 CBU-87 sorties, and later in its life XZ367 was used as an instructional airframe at Cosford, in Shropshire.

7

Jaguar GR 1A XZ358/W (Operation *Granby*), JagDet Muharraq, Bahrain, February 1991

One important role carried out by the JagDet during Operation *Granby* was tactical photo-reconnaissance using both the EMI Jaguar reconnaissance pod and the LOROP. In this view, the aircraft is equipped with the EMI pod, which was attached to the centreline pylon. The external fuel tanks were carried on the underwing pylons during reconnaissance sorties. Just as in the offensive support role, the reconnaissance aircraft were also configured with overwing AIM-9Ls and outboard AN/ALQ-101-10 and Phimat pods. The *DIPLOMATIC SERVICE* nose artwork possibly refers to the Diplomat Hotel where detachment personnel were billeted, although topless service there was probably wishful thinking. The aircraft's mission tally features both bomb silhouettes and 35 mm cameras, the latter obviously denoting reconnaissance sorties.

8

Jaguar GR 1A XX962/X (Operation *Granby*), JagDet Muharraq, Bahrain, February 1991

This is a right-hand side view of the Jaguar depicted in Profile 2, which was decorated with the Arabian woman on the left-hand side. In this view, the unusual additional nose artwork is of the 'Fat Slags' characters from the satirical comic *Viz*. The Phimat chaff pod is also visible on the right outboard wing pylon. The aircraft is loaded with a single CBU-87 on the inner wing pylons. After the Gulf War, during which it completed 17 1000-lb HE bomb and 16 CBU-87 sorties, this aircraft was converted to GR 1B standard and subsequently participated in Operation *Vulcan* over Bosnia-Herzegovina in 1995 (see Profile 18).

9

Jaguar GR 1A XZ375/S (Operation *Granby*), JagDet Muharraq, Bahrain, February 1991

Depicted here with a typical load of four 1000-lb HE bombs, a centreline fuel tank, overwing AIM-9Ls and outboard electronic warfare pods, this aircraft was christened *The avid GUARDIAN Reader*. Apart from the unofficial nose art, Operation *Granby* Jaguars each carried a small black tail letter from N to Z. During work-ups prior to the commencement of fighting in the KTO, XZ375 was flown by Sqn Ldr Mike Rondot, whose name is painted beneath the cockpit and who was not, in fact, an avid reader of *The Guardian* newspaper. The aircraft later participated in the strike on the Serbian airfield at Udbina in 1994 (see Profile 17).

10

Jaguar GR 1A XX725/T (Operation *Granby*), JagDet Muharraq, Bahrain, February 1991

Featuring another character from *Viz* painted by Cpl Paul Robins, this Jaguar was christened *JOHNNY FARTPANTS*. It is shown with a weapon load of two CBU-87s, which featured on 20 sorties flown by the aircraft during Operation *Granby*. In addition, XX725 completed 21 sorties armed with 1000-lb HE bombs and another sortie with CRV7 pods. In June 2007 this aircraft was chosen as the backdrop for the No 6 Sqn disbandment parade at Coningsby, for which it was repainted again in the 'desert pink' scheme, but with the addition of the unit's 'Flying Can Opener' insignia. XX725 was then sent to Cosford for service as an instructional airframe.

11

Jaguar GR 1A XZ356/N (Operation *Granby*), JagDet Muharraq, Bahrain, February 1991

The female figure, christened *MARY ROSE*, on the nose of this Jaguar was the work of Cpl Chris Froome. XZ356 is depicted in the reconnaissance role, equipped with the Vinten Vicon 18-603 LOROP on the centreline, underwing fuel tanks, EW pods and overwing AIM-9Ls. This Jaguar completed six reconnaissance missions, but also flew 24 offensive support missions, including two sorties during which BL755 CBUs bombs were dropped. The aircraft was sold into private ownership in 2006.

12

Jaguar GR 1A XX733/R (Operation *Granby*), JagDet Muharraq, Bahrain, February 1991

The 'pink Spitfire' artwork on this aircraft dated from the last days of the war, being completed just 30 minutes before the ceasefire. It was the favourite of artist Cpl Paul Robins, who recalled, 'I had

decided to base the design on Sqn Ldr [Dave] Bagshaw, the most senior operational Jaguar pilot. My initial idea was to have a typical moustached pilot figure leaning out of a biplane. Those early sketches were not quite right, and after much soul searching and deliberation the desert Spitfire was finally born.' Unfortunately, this aircraft was destroyed in a fatal take-off accident at Coltishall in January 1996.

13

Jaguar GR 1A XZ106/O (Operation *Granby*), JagDet Muharraq, Bahrain, February 1991

This aircraft is depicted carrying CBU-87s, which it expended during 14 sorties in Operation *Granby*. The camera symbols also record the three reconnaissance missions flown by XZ106. All Operation *Granby* Jaguars were painted in 'Desert Pink' ARTF paint over their Cold War grey/green wraparound camouflage, and as the wear and tear of operational flying in the region took its toll, parts of the original finish could be seen. The ARTF paint was also prone to fading in the sun. This aircraft was later modified to GR 3 standard and is preserved at the RAF Manston History Museum in Kent.

14

Jaguar GR 1A XZ364/Q (Operation *Granby*), JagDet Muharraq, Bahrain, February 1991

'About two-and-a-half weeks into the war', recalled Cpl Paul Robins, 'WO Mick Cartwright approached me with a view to painting another "rib tickler" on the nose of XZ364. The design was to be based on the artwork of the station gate guardian Hurricane at Coltishall, on which Hitler is depicted as being given the boot – literally! After several unsuccessful attempts, "Sadman", probably the most well-known of the nose-art drawings, came into being'. The aircraft, boasting an impressive mission tally, is shown here loaded with CBU-87s on the inboard pylons, an AN/ALQ-101-10 pod on the outboard pylon, a centreline fuel tank and overwing AIM-9Ls.

15

Jaguar GR 1A XZ114/FB (Operation *Warden*), Incirlik, Turkey, April 1993

Like the aircraft participating in Operation *Granby*, the Jaguars that deployed to Incirlik were finished in 'Desert Pink' ARTF. Although now devoid of nose art, they retained their individual squadron tail letters, which were prefixed with an 'E' for No 6 Sqn, 'F' for No 41 Sqn and 'G' for No 54 Sqn (the letters 'A' to 'D' had been used by the Brüggen Jaguar Wing). The standard configuration for Operation *Warden* sorties was the same as that used for reconnaissance missions (XZ114 depicted here carrying an EMI pod) during Operation *Granby*, including AN/ALQ-101-10 and Phimat pods and overwing AIM-9Ls.

16

Jaguar GR 1A XZ367/GP (Operation *Deny Flight*), Gioia Del Colle, Italy, November 1994

For operations over the Balkans, the Jaguars were painted in a light grey ARTF finish. In this view, XZ367 is depicted as it was flown by Wg Cdr Tim Kerss during the strike on Udbina airfield on 19 November 1994. The weapon load for this mission was a single 1000-lb HE bomb, since the aiming point was a taxiway and a stick of ordnance delivered accurately would actually have straddled the target. The aircraft is decorated with a *Thunderbird 1* artwork on the nose, and this view is slightly unrealistic in that the Jaguar already carries a single bomb symbol beneath the cockpit recording the successful mission against Udbina.

17

Jaguar GR 1A XZ375/GR (Operation *Deny Flight*), Gioia Del Colle, Italy, November 1994

This Jaguar was flown by Flt Lt Shaun Wildey during the strike on Udbina airfield on 19 November 1994, and it is configured with a single 1000-lb HE bomb, fuel tanks on the inboard pylons, AN/ALQ-101-10 and Phimat pods on the outer pylons and AIM-9Ls on the overwing pylons. The aeroplane had previously been decorated as *The avid GUARDIAN Reader* during Operation *Granby*, but at Gioia Del Colle it was decorated with the carrot and *VEGGIE One* artwork on the nose in reference to Wildey being a vegetarian.

18

Jaguar GR 1B XX962/EK (Operation *Vulcan*), Gioia Del Colle, Italy, August 1995

XX962 had participated in Operation *Granby*, when it was decorated with the Arabian woman and 'Fat Slags' artworks. During Operation *Vulcan* Jaguars flew with the TIALD pod mounted on the centreline and with the by now standard fit of external tanks on the inboard underwing pylons, AN/ALQ-101-10 and Phimat pods on the outboard pylons and overwing AIM-9Ls. The five lightning bolt markings beneath the cockpit record successful TIALD missions completed by the aircraft. It did in fact fly a number of other sorties that were unsuccessful due to issues with the pod or the weather. The aircraft previously served with No 41 Sqn, hence the unit's distinctive Cross of Lorraine insignia in white beneath the lightning bolts. XX962 was scrapped in 2019.

19

Jaguar GR 1B XX748/GK (Operation *Vulcan*), Gioia Del Colle, Italy, August 1995

This aircraft had flown during Operation *Granby*, when it carried the tail letter 'U' but was not decorated with nose art. During Operation *Vulcan* XX748 was flown by Sqn Ldr Alex Muskett and Flt Lt Simon Blake, and it was the Jaguar which carried out the highest number of TIALD sorties. In this view, the Phimat chaff pod mounted on the starboard outer wing pylon is clearly visible. After returning from Gioia Del Colle, the aircraft was transferred to No 6 Sqn, and in 2007, following its retirement from operational service, XX748 became an instructional airframe at Cosford.

20

Jaguar GR 3A XZ113/FD (Operation *Deliberate Guard*), Gioia Del Colle, Italy, July 1997

As in previous operations, the Jaguars that participated in Operation *Deliberate Guard* were finished in grey ARTF paint and carried no unit markings. The stores configuration also remained unchanged, with fuel tanks on the inner pylons, AN/ALQ-101-10 and Phimat pods on the outer pylons and the overwing AIM-9Ls. Although this aircraft is depicted without any offensive ordnance or reconnaissance equipment, the Jaguar GR 3A could also carry a TIALD pod or a Vinten Vicon 18-601 JRP on the centreline for reconnaissance tasks. XZ113 is preserved at the Morayvia museum at Kinloss in Scotland.

21

Jaguar GR 3A XZ357/FK of No 41 Sqn (Operation *Resinate North*), Incirlik, Turkey, February 1999

By the late 1990s Jaguars were finished in an overall grey scheme that was a slightly darker shade than the ARTF paint previously applied to aircraft on detached operations. During the return of the Jaguar force to Incirlik for Operation *Resinate North* in the late 1990s, the aircraft also retained their unit markings, in this case those of No 41 Sqn. The red and white stripes and Cross of Lorraine markings originated when the squadron flew Hunters in the 1950s. This Jaguar is shown in its operational configuration, with a Vinten Vicon 18-601 JRP on the centreline. XZ357 was acquired by Piet Smits in 2008 for his museum at Baarlo in the Netherlands, and in 2021 it was sold on to a private collector.

22

Jaguar GR 3A XX720/GB of No 54 Sqn (Operation *Resinate North*), Incirlik, Turkey, September 2002

This aircraft, depicted as it was configured for reconnaissance missions into the Northern NFZ over Iraq, is finished in the colours of No 54 Sqn. The blue and yellow chequerboard markings were first worn by Hunters of the squadron in the 1950s. Although the overwing pylons are fitted, AAMs were not routinely carried as there was no perceived fighter threat. However, the Phimat chaff pod is still attached to the outer stores pylon beneath the starboard wing and AN/ALE-40 flare dispensers are visible forward of the ventral strakes.

The retractable refuelling probe is extended as Jaguar XZ115 closes up to the tanker for air-to-air refuelling during a training sortie in late 1990. It is carrying an EMI reconnaissance pod on the centreline pylon. In the background, a Tornado GR 1 awaits its turn to refuel. XZ115 was later converted to GR 3A standard, and its survives as an instructional airframe at Cosford (*Crown Copyright/MoD*)

INDEX

Page locators in **bold** refer to illustrations.
Colour plate locators are marked 'cp.', with page
locators for plate and commentary in brackets.